DATE DUE			

8570

979.4   Reinstedt, Randall
R   A.

Tales and treasures
of California's
missions

Tales and Treasures

of California's Missions

Missions of California

San Francisco Solano ●

San Rafael Arcangel ●

SAN FRANCISCO

San Francisco de Asis

● San Jose

● Santa Cruz

● San Juan Bautista

Santa Clara de Asis

● Nuestra Senora de la Soledad

San Antonio de Padua

San Carlos Borromeo
del Rio Carmelo

● San Miguel Arcangel

● San Luis Obispo de Tolosa

Santa Barbara

La Purisima Concepcion
● Santa Ines

San Buenaventura ● ● San Fernando Rey de Espana

LOS ANGELES

● San Juan Capistrano

● San Luis Rey de Francia

San Gabriel Arcangel **SAN DIEGO**

San Diego de Alcala

Tales and Treasures

of California's Missions

Randall A. Reinstedt

Illustrated by Ed Greco

Ghost Town Publications
Carmel, California

Randall A. Reinstedt's
History & Happenings of California Series
Ghost Town Publications
P.O. Drawer 5998
Carmel, CA 93921

10 9 8 7 6 5 4 3

Manufactured in the United States of America

Library of Congress Catalog Number 92-73253
ISBN 0-933818-24-6 Hardcover
ISBN 0-933818-79-3 Softcover

Edited by John Bergez
Cover design and illustrations by Ed Greco

Contents

Introduction: Follow the Mustard Seeds

This is a book about seven of California's famous missions. It is not a book that tells you all the facts about our state's colorful Mission Period. Instead, it is a book of tales and treasures—real treasures, like bandits' gold and pirates' booty, and also the "treasures" of memories that have gathered around these special places. For, as you will see, the missions continued to be sites of interesting happenings long after the padres and Indians had gone.

It is only fitting that I begin this book of mission tales by sharing a short story with you. The story is a legend— meaning that we cannot be sure that the events that take place in it really happened as they are described. Still, it is a story with a special meaning for me. It is about the famous Mission Trail.

Long ago, the story goes, when the Spanish padres came to Alta California and started the chain of churches that stretch up and down the coast, there were no signposts to mark their path. As time went on, and the chain grew, the missions made convenient stopping-off places for visiting padres and others who passed their way. However, these wayside stops were of little value to travelers if they couldn't be found.

Fortunately, the legend states, the enterprising padres had brought mustard seeds from Spain, which they dropped along the route. When the seeds grew into flowering mustard stalks, they marked the trail with a blaze of color. This pathway bordered in brilliant yellow is said to have guided wayfarers from church to church—even at night. In this way the mustard plants helped to make El Camino Real (the Royal Road, also referred to as the Public Highway or the King's Highway) one of the most popular and beautiful trails in the territory.

Today flowering mustard stalks are seen in much of California. When history buffs view their vivid color, they may think back to another time and ponder the plight of the padres as they plodded along a barely visible path, dropping mustard seeds as they went so others could follow.

Like the mustard plants, today the story of California and its missions has spread far and wide. Sometimes when I think about this book, I like to compare it to the padres as they scattered the seeds. For with this work I hope to spread interesting anecdotes about the missions, combined with tempting tales of treasures and fascinating accounts of the way it used to be.

Some of these stories come from the exciting time known as California's Mission Period—a time of turmoil and triumph, happiness and heartache . . . not only for the padres and Spanish soldiers and settlers, but for the California Indians who peopled the land before it was explored by Europeans.

But the story of the missions doesn't end with the Mission Period. The padres, you see, had chosen their mission sites well, spacing them out conveniently for travelers and often building them on locations that had many advantages. Some of the missions, for example, were built near good places for ports and military outposts, such as San Diego, Monterey, and San Francisco bays. Whole towns, and later sizable cities, grew up near many of the padres' churches, including San Diego, Los Angeles, Santa Barbara, San Jose, and San Francisco. In fact, if you could follow the mustard plant trail today, you would travel through several of the most important cities in California.

As a result, even as some of the missions fell into decay, events continued to happen around the sites the padres had chosen. In this way the missions continued to play a role in California history that the padres could never have imagined.

This book tells about many of these events. Besides padres and Indians, you will read about lost treasures, forgotten mines, bandits and pirates, and even tragic shipwrecks. These happenings and more are all a part of the continuing history that began with the missions.

So, like the wayfarers of old, follow the mustard seeds from page to page, and together we'll share in the excitement of California's colorful past.

Mission San Diego

Mission San Diego de Alcala was the first
mission to be established. It was founded in
1769 by Padre Junipero Serra.

Mission
San Diego

Our journey begins with California's southernmost mission, and the first church to be built in Alta (Upper) California. Even though many of the missions had problems in their early years, the establishment of Mission San Diego was among the most difficult. Despair, disease, and death were only part of the problems that faced Padre Junipero Serra, the leader of the mission movement, and his co-workers. Among Serra's many worries were the shortage of food and supplies, the inability to seek help from neighboring churches and presidios (military posts), and attacks by Indians defending their homeland.

It is little wonder that at one point Captain Gaspar de Portola, the governor and military leader of the founding expedition, considered abandoning the settlement and returning to Mexico. Portola learned of the desperate situation at San Diego upon his return from an unsuccessful attempt to find Monterey Bay, a northerly inlet where the second mission was to be built. Padre Serra, however, refused to give up. Convinced that an expected supply ship would arrive, and that conditions would improve, he pleaded with Portola for more time.

Admiring the padre's faith and determination, Portola agreed to wait until St. Joseph's Day—March 19, 1770—which was nine days away. So it was that the future of Spain's involvement in Alta California depended upon the arrival of the supply ship, the *San Antonio.*

Anxiously, the Spanish at San Diego scanned the horizon for signs of a sail. As the days came and went, and no vessel was spotted, Portola proceeded with plans to return to Mexico.

When St. Joseph's Day dawned, still no ship was in sight. Most agreed that time had run out for San Diego and its troubled mission. Soon preparations were complete for an early morning departure the next day. Yet Serra refused to give up hope. Then, as late afternoon approached, a cry suddenly echoed throughout the colony. Sails were sighted on the horizon . . . only to be lost in an ocean mist.

Even though no ship arrived, so impressed was Portola at this remarkable event that he agreed to postpone his departure. Four days later the *San Antonio* made its way into San Diego Bay. Upon questioning the crew, the Spanish learned that the phantom vessel they had seen was, indeed, the supply ship. The ship had not put in at San Diego because its captain had orders calling for him to meet Portola in Monterey. However, the vessel had developed problems on the way up the coast and had returned to San Diego for repairs.

So, thanks to the supply ship's misadventure, Spanish California was saved! And, because of the chance sighting of a ghostly sail in the mist on St. Joseph's Day, California's famed Mission Period was given a second chance.

As time went on, California's first church prospered, becoming one of the wealthiest of the coastal churches. As with many of the other missions, Padre Serra's little settlement started a chain of events that continues to this day. The bay that gave shelter to the *San Antonio* later became the site of an important U.S. Navy base, and today the mission marks the location of one of California's largest and most popular cities.

Along the way, many fascinating events took place around the site of Serra's mission. In 1822 Mexico gained its independence from Spain, and in 1825 San Diego became the temporary capital of California. While headquartered there, Governor Jose Maria Echeandia was visited by the famous Yankee trapper and mountain man, Jedediah Strong Smith.

Smith was the first American to travel overland into Mexican California. Arriving in either late 1826 or early 1827, he was given a chilly welcome by Echeandia, and only after some tense moments was he allowed to purchase supplies and take his leave. Unfortunately for Smith and his men (who waited for him at Mission San Gabriel to the north), they were discouraged from leaving California via the route they wished to take. (Incidentally, when Smith finally did venture east, he became the first Yankee to cross the Sierra Nevada.)

A little over a year after Smith's visit to San Diego, in March, 1828, a second group of Americans succeeded in making an overland crossing. However, instead of being warmly greeted by the padres at the Baja (Lower) California mission of Santa Catalina, they were put in the guardhouse. From there they were taken to San Diego.

Governor Echeandia was suspicious of the Yankees—especially the group's leaders, Sylvester Pattie (former Kentuckian, ranger, lumberman, and trapper) and his teenage son, James Ohio Pattie. Thinking they might be spies, he tore up their passports and had them placed in separate prison cells. Being imprisoned was bad enough, but Sylvester Pattie was already unwell because of the many hardships the party had suffered during their exhausting trip across the desert to Mission Santa Catalina. Sylvester couldn't stand up to the poor food and harsh treatment the Yankees received at San Diego. Sadly, he died in his cell.

After the death of his father, James Pattie endured several months of cruel captivity. While he was imprisoned, he was given an opportunity to help the governor. Pattie had learned a little Spanish while in the area of New Mexico. Now he used this knowledge by serving as an interpreter, translating items written in English and dealing with seafarers from foreign lands.

However, it wasn't until later that Pattie was in a position to bid for his freedom. A deadly epidemic of smallpox was threatening the province, particularly along the north coast. Pattie had brought some smallpox vaccine with him, and it proved to be his passport to freedom. The young trapper and the governor worked out a deal. In exchange for his release and the release of his companions, Pattie agreed to travel up and down the coast vaccinating everyone he encountered.

There is much more to this story than I can tell here, but here are a few facts that indicate why James Ohio Pattie's stay in California was so remarkable. First, it is said that he saved the population from the smallpox epidemic by vaccinating thousands of people. While that accomplishment is enough by itself to make him a hero, he and his father are also remembered because their expedition pioneered a new route to the coast. Finally, after returning to the United States, the young Pattie wrote a book about his adventures that has contributed to our knowledge of the southwestern territory through which he passed.

The territory crossed by James Pattie is rich in legend and lore, and fascinating stories are told about it and the California desert. One of my favorite tales is linked to San Diego and tells of a treasure ship that was lost—not at sea, but in the desert sand! What was a ship of any kind doing in the desert? Read on, because that is part of the story.

It seems that in the late 1700s, not long after San Diego got its start, a Spanish galleon filled with treasures from the other side of the ocean was caught in a fierce Pacific storm. Blown off its course, the ship was unable to reach the port of Acapulco, far down the west coast of Mexico. Instead the crew sought a safe anchorage at Guaymas, inside the more sheltered waters of the Baja California peninsula.

Unfortunately, the storm sent giant waves up the Gulf of California. Instead of dropping anchor at Guaymas, the vessel was driven to the upper end of the inlet—and beyond. So huge and powerful were the waves that the raging sea washed over the gulf's north shore and into the desert flats, carrying the galleon with it!

The astonished captain soon found his battered ship far from familiar waters. As the storm subsided and the sea receded, a lake was formed in the desert. Round and round the landlocked lake the captain sailed, but try as he might he couldn't find an outlet.

Realizing he was stranded in this small inland sea, the captain feared that his ship would be left "high and dry" when the water either evaporated or soaked into the sand. In desperation he sent several members of his crew trudging across the desert in search of help. Apparently, only one man survived the journey. Upon staggering into the tiny seaside settlement of San Diego, he told his story, and then he too died. A relief party set out in search of the galleon, but neither the lake nor the vessel could be found.

As the years came and went, the shifting sands of the desert are said to have covered the ship—only to uncover it again at the whim of Mother Nature. Over time Indians and other travelers claimed to have glimpsed the remains of a vessel partly buried in the desert sands, but many doubt whether it was the Spanish treasure galleon that they saw —or whether such an event even took place.

If the tale of the landlocked galleon seems improbable, consider this: it isn't the only account of a lost treasure ship in the California desert! A second tale tells of a Spanish captain who fished and traded for pearls in the Gulf of California in the early 1600s. After stocking his vessel with the valuable gems, he proceeded up the gulf. Reaching the northern end of the inlet, he saw a narrow channel. Thinking it might be the entrance to the fabled Straits of Anian (a water route to the Atlantic Ocean), the captain succeeded in sailing up the channel. Soon he came upon a large body of water. As he explored this inland sea, a flash flood raged out of the mountains and blocked the channel. With no other exit, the captain and his crew were forced to abandon their ship—and most of the pearls!

More than 150 years later, the Spanish explorer Juan Bautista de Anza led a famous expedition that opened a land route between Sonora, Mexico, and Alta California. According to one story, the muleteer of the expedition discovered the remains of the long-lost pearl ship. He couldn't believe his eyes. Amid the sun-bleached bones of the ship, he found a vast quantity of pearls!

Carrying as many of the precious gems as he could, the muleteer deserted the expedition and headed west. Upon making his way to Mission San Diego, he rested, regained his strength, and thought about the magnificent hoard of pearls still waiting to be claimed. Befriending some Indians, he attempted to return with them to the site—but he was never able to relocate the vessel.

Are the tales true? Was there really a landlocked galleon or a "pearl ship" abandoned on the desert floor? Many history buffs are doubtful, but tales of these and other ships lost in the sand persist to this day.

In working our way back from the desert to San Diego, it is fitting that we stop at the Chapel of Santa Ysabel. Santa Ysabel is described as an *asistencia,* or outpost, of Mission San Diego. Established in 1818, in a northeasterly direction from its mother church, the small inland outpost was quite successful in its early years. However, as the Mission Period began its decline, priestly visits to the outlying church became rare. Soon the buildings began to fall into disrepair. By 1852 a visitor to the site reported that only a few structures were still standing, and the once-inviting chapel was roofless.

To some this seems to sum up the history of Santa Ysabel, but others—treasure buffs included—know there is more to the story.

Perhaps the best-known treasure tale connected with this church is the story of its lost bells. Even though they may not be worth much when compared to the cargo of a Spanish treasure galleon, to those who love history they are priceless.

The two bells are said to have been purchased by Indians from a mission in Baja California. The Indians then began the difficult task of transporting them to Santa Ysabel. Once in place the bells were used to call the faithful to prayer. When the chapel began to deteriorate, the Indians mounted the bells on a wooden rack in the churchyard. Here they remained until the 1920s, when they mysteriously disappeared.

Some say souvenir hunters took the bells, while others guess that they were stolen and sold for scrap. Still others wonder whether Indians claimed the bells and hid them in the nearby mountains . . . where other church valuables are said to be stashed!

This brings us to a second Santa Ysabel treasure tale. About the time Mexico gained its independence from Spain (1822), the padres were very concerned about what would become of the missions. Supposedly, the padres from Mission San Diego (and perhaps other El Camino Real churches) took their golden altar ornaments and other objects of value to Santa Ysabel for safekeeping.

After collecting quite a hoard of church artifacts, the local padres are said to have buried them somewhere nearby, possibly on a hillside near an old stage stop. There the items remain hidden to this day.

Unfortunately, some people find the tale difficult to accept, particularly when they learn of an Indian legend stating that Indians can sometimes see a flame (or "pillar of light") at the spot where the valuables are buried. However, there is also a second legend which suggests that a mysterious object was left at the site by shamans to watch over the treasure. (Shamans are special individuals who often are thought to have close contact with the spirit world. They are also usually skilled in curing diseases, and some Indian groups refer to them as medicine men.) Incidentally, there are those who think that the mission bells and the other church artifacts are buried at the same site!

If these stories have whetted your appetite for treasure seeking, but you hesitate to dig where a mysterious objcct may keep watch, let me tell you one more tale about a treasure in the Santa Ysabel area. Again, this brief story may be little more than a legend. But if your bags are packed anyway, you might as well keep your eyes peeled for a deerskin pouch the size of a man's head. According to an aged padre's tale, sometime around the 1850s three miners were killed in the area. A leather pack they had stashed before they met their deaths was never found. Supposedly the head-sized sack was filled with gold in the form of nuggets, flakes, and dust. In concluding, the tale hints that the gold remains hidden somewhere in the hills west of Santa Ysabel.

For more treasure tales, let's return to the area around Mission San Diego. Since even before the days of Padre Serra, much of the region's history has been linked with the sea, so it is only natural that some of its tales of lost wealth would be about valuables beneath the Pacific. One of the best-known of these accounts is the story of the Spanish ship *Trinidad*, which was lost somewhere north of San Diego around 1540. Over the years there has been much speculation about the loss of this vessel, with estimates of her treasure seeming to fall and rise with the tides. Educated guesses have placed the value of her cargo at somewhere between four and twelve million dollars' worth of coins, gold, and assorted artifacts!

Coincidentally, the *Trinidad* wasn't the only Spanish vessel to be lost off the southern California shore in or about 1540. Tales also tell of the galleon *Santo Domingo*, which is said to have met her end approximately five miles off Escondido Creek, slightly north of San Diego. A "measly" three million dollars in gold and silver is reported to have been aboard her when she went down.

Closer to San Diego, an old sea captain's treasure is rumored to be buried a few hundred feet above the high water mark. According to the tale, in the early 1800s a Captain Brown from New England was making his way up the California coast when he became suspicious of sails in the distance. Thinking that pirates might be tracking his vessel, and not wanting to give up the $50,000 in gold he had aboard, the captain guided his ship toward a nearby beach. (The beach is reported to be in the vicinity of present-day Coronado, slightly south of the entrance of San Diego Bay.) Next he had the treasure loaded on a small boat and rowed to shore. After the gold was buried, Brown continued up the coast. Along the way he learned that the sails he had seen were not those of a pirate. However, Brown knew that Spanish vessels were patrolling the California waters, hoping to discourage foreign trade—which is what he was involved with. To play it safe, he decided to leave the gold buried where it was and return for it at a later date.

Sadly for the Boston-based captain, his ship was lost and, apparently, he was lost along with it. Interestingly, however, Brown had left a map that showed the location of the buried gold. Eventually the map made its way to his family, along with his other belongings. Living on the other side of the country, the relatives were unable to act on the map when they received it. But many years later, during the great California Gold Rush (mid-1800s), a family member who had joined the rush west detoured to San Diego with the map. Unfortunately, try as he might he was unable to find the treasure.

While this is a nice way to end the tale—as it gives us another sizable fortune to think about—I can't help but wonder whether other people had copies of the map . . . and who may have searched for the treasure long before the Gold Rush got its start.

While we're in the area of Coronado, I think it is appropriate to mention an account of another buried treasure that appeared in a local newspaper (the *San Diego Union*) more than one hundred years ago. Headlined "Dollars in the Dust," the article told of a 12-year-old Coronado girl who found an abundance of silver dollars in her backyard. It seems that by merely "kicking up" the dirt she revealed the coins. Soon the word spread, and several treasure seekers arrived on the scene. However, no matter how hard the new arrivals tried, the girl was the only one to achieve success.

As for where the money came from, no one could say. Oddly enough, the coins were scattered over a wide expanse (sometimes they were found more than 50 feet apart), and only a single dollar was found at a time. It seemed that the coins had been purposely sprinkled about the yard. Why anyone would try to keep money hidden by scattering it about a yard in this way remains a mystery.

Our last San Diego tale returns us to Alta California's historic first mission for another story that involves hidden church artifacts—and, just for spice, a lost gold mine besides!

The tale begins in mission days, at a time when the padres and Indians were at peace. One lazy afternoon, a padre noticed a small Indian boy playing with some arrowheads. The boy was well known to the priest, as he often helped around the mission. After watching the lad awhile, the padre asked if he could see one of the arrowheads. Upon examining the prized point, the priest was impressed with the workmanship and the beauty of the quartz from which it was made. But what really caught his eye were the streaks of gold that ran through it! After inspecting the other points, he realized they had all come from the same source.

Excited about the gold, the padre questioned the boy and learned that he had obtained the arrowheads from the chief of a mountain village near El Cajon, east of San Diego. The padre shared the news—and the arrowheads—with his fellow priest, and the two padres made plans to talk to the chief. Accompanied by a small group of mission-based soldiers, the boy was sent to tell the Indian chief that the church fathers wished to speak to him.

Shortly the soldiers and the boy returned to the mission, together with the chief and several of his villagers. The chief informed the priests that on El Cajon Mountain, behind the Indian village, there was an abundance of rock similar to what he had used to make the points that had excited the padres. Unfortunately, the chief added, the rock had too much "yellow" in it to make it useful for arrowheads.

Of course, it was the soft yellow rock that the padres were interested in! Delighted with the chief's report, they asked the Indians to swear that they would keep the location of the "soft rock" a secret.

The fathers and the chief then worked out a deal. The padres promised to have the mission soldiers watch over the village to ensure that its people lived in peace. In exchange for this protection, the chief agreed to fill several rawhide bags with yellow rock prior to each full moon. Once a month, when the moon was round, a muleteer from the church would visit the village at night in the company of the lad who had originally shown the arrowheads to the priest. The rawhide sacks would then be loaded onto the backs of the mules and taken to the church, where the padres stashed the gold in a secret room.

After each of these trips the padres began the task of separating the gold from the quartz. Eventually they filled several chests with gold and had them taken to the bay by wagon and placed aboard a Spanish vessel bound for Acapulco. At Acapulco the valuable cargo was again loaded on a wagon and transported to the church treasury in Mexico City.

Not all of the gold found its way to Mexico City, however. According to the document from which this account came, the priests kept enough of the gold to make beautiful decorations for the interior of the mission. These adornments were admired by all who saw them, and are said to have added greatly to the beauty of the church.

It is these decorations, along with the secret source of the padres' gold, that makes this story a treasure tale. In 1822, after Mexico gained its independence from Spain, the padres at San Diego knew they could no longer keep their promise of protecting the village from which they got the gold. With this in mind, they told the chief that the shipments must stop and that his people must conceal the mine in such a way that no one would know what had taken place there.

When this was accomplished, the fathers breathed easier and continued their work at the mission. However, with the passing of Spanish rule, conditions at the mission began to deteriorate. It was only a matter of time before the buildings started to crumble, the flocks began to dwindle, and production dropped off. Depressed and discouraged, one of the priests took sick and died, while the other bravely carried on.

By 1846 California history was undergoing another dramatic change as the United States and Mexico went to war. During the war Mexican soldiers moved into the church compound. When the remaining padre saw the way they looked at the mission's golden ornaments, he decided the time had come to hide the objects.

One dark night, when the soldiers were not about, the priest gathered four of his trusted helpers (including the boy who had first shown the yellow rock to the padre, and who had long since grown to manhood). Together the padre and the Indians took the gold and treasured service pieces from the church and placed them in a chest. The Indians then headed for the nearby hills on foot, carrying the heavy chest with them. By the time dawn came, and the valued artifacts were discovered missing, the Indians watched from a distance as the soldiers set out on horseback to find the items—and the thieves who took them!

Realizing their trail would soon be found, and with the heavy chest slowing their escape, the weary Indians knew they must soon find a place to hide the gold. As they continued in the direction of a "black mountain" that rose from the foothills ahead of them, they spotted a crevice in the rock that was about the size of the chest. The opening was partly covered by a large flat rock. With the soldiers coming ever closer, the quick-thinking Indians removed the ropes and poles they had used to carry the chest and shoved it into the crevice. With a mighty heave, they slid the flat rock over the opening and hurriedly wiped away all signs of activity with branches from nearby bushes. Melting away into the brush that dotted the hillsides, the Indians eluded the frustrated soldiers—who never found the chest containing the mission treasures.

To this day, the chest remains hidden, and the location of the mine that produced the soft yellow rock is a secret that lies buried with the Indian villagers. At least, that is what the tale claims—a tale to be treasured as part of the storied history of Mission San Diego.

Mission San Gabriel

Mission San Gabriel Arcangel was the fourth mission to be established. It was founded in 1771 by Padres Angel Somera and Pedro Cambon (under the guidance of Padre Junipero Serra).

Mission
San Gabriel

What went through the minds of Padres Angel Somera and Pedro Cambon on that September day when they founded the fourth mission in Alta California? What vision of the future did they see in the sun-kissed, empty spaces around them, a few miles from the river the Spanish called the Porciuncula?

Perhaps they pictured a mission church surrounded by shady orchards of fruit trees and vineyards bursting with grapes for making wine. Maybe they imagined herds of livestock grazing and yellow fields of grain against the backdrop of the rugged San Gabriel Mountains. But it seems safe to say that in their wildest dreams they never pictured a sprawling metropolis of more than three million people from the four corners of the earth!

Yet that is exactly what grew from the seed that the padres planted when they established Mission San Gabriel Arcangel on September 8, 1771. More than 200 years later, the "City of Angels" that grew up near the little mission covers more than 400 square miles and boasts more people than any other city in the United States.

Of course, such a huge and important city is often in the news. Luckily for the newscasters, its original name has been shortened to just two words, Los Angeles. Can you imagine radio and television announcers saying *El Pueblo de Nuestra Senora la Reina de Los Angeles de la Porciuncula* every time they referred to this great city? (Translated, the name means The Town of Our Lady, Queen of the Angels of the Porciuncula.)

Back in the days of the padres, San Gabriel gained its own share of fame by becoming one of their most successful missions—perhaps the most prosperous in the entire mission chain. The mission boasted extensive vineyards, which produced an estimated 50,000 gallons of California's best wine each year. Its production of grain was almost always tops among the missions, and its many crops included corn, peas, lentils, garbanzos, barley, and beans. It even had its own factory, which supplied most of the missions with soap.

Perhaps the best feature of the mission, though, was its orchards and olive groves. Besides olives, the fruits that were grown included oranges, lemons, pears, peaches, apples, and figs. Visitors to the mission must have been impressed to see gardens and orchards that covered hundreds of acres and featured more than 2,000 trees! With such extensive crops and fruit production, it's little wonder that Mission San Gabriel came to be known as the "Mother of California Agriculture."

Protecting much of this property from uninvited guests (both human and animal) was a wall of cactus that grew, in places, more than ten feet high. Interestingly, parts of the cactus hedge and orchard can be seen to this day around the town of San Gabriel, which today is a suburb of Los Angeles. (The mission itself is located about nine miles northeast of downtown Los Angeles.)

As to livestock holdings, the enterprising padres and Indians of San Gabriel proved equally successful. Most of the thousands of animals they maintained were cattle, which were branded with the letter "T." The "T" stood for *temblores* (earthquakes)—a fitting name, since there were several earthquakes in the area during the mission's early years. In fact, a nearby river had already acquired the name Rio de los Temblores (River of Earthquakes). The river got its name when a party of Spanish explorers in the area were shaken by four strong quakes on the same day!

As with many of the early churches, San Gabriel's original location was eventually abandoned. The main reason for the move was flooding. The new site, approximately five miles away, was higher and drier. It was at this location that an imposing fortress-like mission building was constructed. Unlike any other structure in California, the building was modeled after the Cordova cathedral in Spain. In use to this day, the church continues to impress those who visit it. Among other interesting features it boasts an outstanding museum filled with priceless treasures from the past.

Counted among the treasures—at least from my point of view—are the many stories that are told about the mission and about the communities that grew up around it. Among the tales is one which states that the church grounds were once used as a shipyard. While it may seem odd for a mission to be in the boat-building business, it seems even odder for that mission to have been San Gabriel, considering that the church was more than two dozen miles from the sea!

Nevertheless, according to this story, in 1830 the 99-ton schooner *Guadalupe* was constructed near the mission. Upon completion it was taken apart and transported to the port town of San Pedro. Here, on the shores of the Pacific, it was rebuilt and launched. Proving seaworthy, the vessel soon set sail for San Blas, Mexico, with a load of mission goods.

Although I hate to spoil the story of such an impressive undertaking, I should mention that another version indicates that the ship *wasn't* constructed on the church grounds after all. According to this account, the vessel's timbers were cut from a canyon 50 miles away and hauled to San Pedro, where the *Guadalupe* was built. The story also suggests that the ship was smaller than the 99-ton vessel mentioned in the first account. Interestingly, the carpenter who built the craft is billed as a "reformed American pirate" who arrived in California aboard privateer Hippolyte Bouchard's ship (see the Carmel Mission chapter for more information on Bouchard). Joseph Chapman was his name, and in addition to his talent as a carpenter, the padres made good use of his blacksmithing and doctoring skills as well.

With the mention of Joseph Chapman, a second individual comes to mind. This person was a Baja California Indian who left Mission San Gabriel with plans of returning to his home. According to most sources, the Indian was known as Sebastian, and accompanying him on his escape were members of his family. (Whether it was his wife and child, or his wife and parents, sources disagree.)

Heading east instead of south in an attempt to avoid soldiers who might be sent after them, the determined Indians set out across the burning desert. Suffering terrible hardships along the way, Sebastian succeeded in reaching the Colorado River. Sadly, he was the only one to make it out of the desert alive.

After his harrowing experience, Sebastian met the Spanish explorer Juan Bautista de Anza, who was seeking a land route between Sonora, Mexico, and Alta California. Soon an understanding was reached, and Sebastian agreed to lead the Anza party back across the desert. This successful crossing took place in 1774, when there were five missions in Alta California. The crossing caused much rejoicing at San Gabriel. Not only did it open a new route to Mexico, but it helped to ensure the success of Alta California's remote mission outposts.

Two other individuals who often crop up when the San Gabriel area is discussed are a couple of fellows with the same first name. One of them is Tiburcio Tapia, who is said to have been a leading citizen in the early days of Los Angeles. An account of Tapia's lost wealth will come later in this chapter. The other Tiburcio is bandit chieftain Tiburcio Vasquez.

The notorious Vasquez is considered California's second most famous badman. Only Joaquin Murrieta was ahead of him on California lawmen's list of "most wanted" men. (You will learn more about Murrieta later in this book.)

Born in Monterey in 1835, Vasquez began his career of crime when he was a teenager. While perhaps not as blood-thirsty as some of the Golden State's lesser-known bandits, he didn't take a back seat to anyone when it came to ranging far and wide. Among the areas he chose to operate in was Los Angeles County. It was also here that he often hid out.

Outlaw hideouts and lost treasures seem to go hand in hand. Among the Vasquez gang's favorite Los Angeles County hideouts is one that has become known as Vasquez Rocks. Also called Robber's Roost, this interesting rock formation is located high on a ridge in the Escondido Canyon area, west of the community of Acton. Over the years several fortune hunters are rumored to have tried their luck on the high ridge, but no important finds have been reported.

About two miles from Vasquez Rocks, also in Escondido Canyon, are a series of small caves that have been carved by the wind and rain. Legends state that Vasquez used the maze-like caves as a hideout because no posse could—or would—track him there. Appropriately, the caves gained their names from this feared outlaw leader. To this day stories circulate about the area, stating that bandit loot is stashed in the vicinity of Vasquez Caves.

Another Los Angeles County stronghold that the Vasquez gang frequented is north of the city of Monrovia. Residents of the region probably know the area best as East and West Chilao (within the Charlton Chilao Recreation Area).

Part of this property is a wilderness region of rock and timber that seems ideally suited for a bandit hideout—especially when you consider its secret trails and fortress-like rocks. As with the Vasquez Caves, posses were hesitant to pursue the badmen into the area. Oh, yes, the Vasquez gang is rumored to have buried ample amounts of stolen wealth there!

Closer to San Gabriel, between Los Angeles and the mission, an old road led through a hilly region. During the early days this wagon route was heavily traveled. In the foothills, near the road, Vasquez is said to have stashed a treasure of gold coins. Many years later a boy reportedly found a scattering of coins in the area. Unfortunately, he couldn't pinpoint the spot where he had picked them up. Today the district is almost completely covered with homes, causing fortune hunters to seek other sites in which to dig.

Also near San Gabriel—and perhaps a more likely spot to look—a $40,000 treasure is said to have been lost. According to this account, in April, 1874, the Vasquez gang attacked the headquarters of the Repetto Ranch, located south of the mission (in the vicinity of present-day Monterey Park). Capturing Alessandro Repetto, the owner of the ranch, the horseback gangsters demanded his money. Repetto swore that all his money was in a Los Angeles bank. Not giving up so easily, the robbers ordered the rancher to sign a note to the bank requesting a large sum of money. While a boy hurried to the bank with the note, members of the bandit crew who thought Repetto was lying began torturing him. Finally giving in, the rancher handed over two bags filled with $40,000 in gold and silver!

Meanwhile, officials at the bank became suspicious of the boy's note and notified the sheriff. The frightened lad soon revealed what had happened at the ranch. Quickly the sheriff gathered a posse and headed for the scene.

Unfortunately for the cause of justice, the robbers sensed that something was wrong. Having already obtained what they were after, they decided to exit the area. But the bags of money slowed them down, and they decided to stop and hide the loot.

Not long after, a passerby told Repetto he had seen a group of men who appeared to be in a great hurry come to a sudden halt and bury something in some nearby woods on the ranch property. It is said that Repetto spent many years looking for the buried treasure, but all of his efforts were in vain.

Today, although much of the 5,000-acre Repetto Ranch is built upon, rumors say that some of the original wooded areas remain the same. If you decide to go on a treasure hunt, though, take an adult with you—and be sure to get permission from the property owners before beginning your expedition.

Incidentally, about a month after the Repetto robbery Tiburcio Vasquez was captured within easy riding distance of both the Repetto Ranch and Mission San Gabriel. When he was arrested, the bandit king was nearly broke. Reportedly, however, he hinted that "if a deal could be made" he could quickly come up with a sizable sum of money. Could it be that Vasquez was thinking of the Repetto Ranch loot?

Now, as promised, let me tell you about another Tiburcio, and another lost treasure. This tale takes us to an area east of Los Angeles known to old-timers as the Rancho Cucamonga Tract. The name Cucamonga came from an Indian village that was on the site when the Spanish first came to Alta California. Padres from Mission San Gabriel sometimes visited the area and worked with the Indians who lived there.

In 1839 the land that formed the Cucamonga tract was granted by the Mexican government to Tiburcio Tapia. A well-known citizen in the early days of Los Angeles, Tapia was also a former soldier and public official. After receiving the grant, he built a huge adobe house—more like a fortress than a residence—on the tract's highest hill. From atop the hill he could keep an eye on his vast holdings and withstand attacks from Cucamonga Indians who were unhappy with the way he had taken control of their land.

What makes Tapia's story a treasure tale is the hoard of valuables (probably consisting mostly of gold coins) that he had acquired over a period of years. Some sources suggest the treasure also included contributions from others—money that was supposed to help finance the building of a new chapel on the ranch.

What became of the chest that contained this wealth is a lasting mystery. Apparently, after the United States took control of the territory in 1846, Tapia and many other California ranchers feared that their land and wealth might be taken from them. With this in mind, it is said, Tapia buried the chest for safekeeping. Unfortunately for his heirs—and happily for future treasure seekers—several sources say that he died without divulging the secret of where the chest was hidden.

Some seem to think that Tapia buried the bonanza under the floorboards of his huge house. However, many searches have been made where the structure once stood, and nothing has been found. Others believe that the chest was stashed on the ranch grounds, but over the years a number of people have looked for it without success.

With the fortune still missing, another account begins to take on more meaning. According to this story, after the U.S. takeover, news reached Tapia that a large American force was moving into the area. Loading his treasure on an oxcart, Tapia pointed the oxen toward Los Angeles . . . or San Pedro . . . or maybe even San Bernardino (take your pick, as different sources hint at different destinations).

Whatever the destination was, when Tapia was next seen he was very weak—and the oxcart was empty! As in the first account, this story says that Tapia died before he could disclose the chest's hiding place.

Or did he? According to still another version, before Tapia died he was able to whisper the whereabouts of the treasure to a trusted companion. Unfortunately, the message was unclear, and about all his companion could understand was that the chest was buried in a stand of timber beneath an "elbow-shaped limb" of a giant sycamore tree. The woods Tapia supposedly spoke of are thought to have been found, and fortune hunters dug several holes looking for the missing treasure, without success. (The site is now occupied by the city of Pomona.) Today—thanks to the many accounts that have been written about it—the tale is widely known and theories continue to crop up as to where Tapia's lost treasure might be.

The mention of Pomona brings to mind another case of lost riches. This story concerns an Indian gold mine located in the nearby San Gabriel Mountains, not far from the community of Claremont (Pomona's neighbor to the north). The Indians who worked the mine were from Mission San Gabriel. Although small quantities of gold have since been found in the canyons north of Claremont, the mine's site has eluded searchers for more than a century and a half.

Tales of a lost mine remind me of another story of Indian gold in the San Gabriel area. Approximately a dozen miles northeast of the mission is a rugged region known as Fish Canyon. (Fish Canyon empties into the San Gabriel

Wash, which is often thought of as part of the San Gabriel River system. Today it is usually dry, but it is a threat to flood when heavy rains hit.) According to the story, more than 100 years ago (probably in the early 1880s), an Indian woman was herding goats in the region. Suddenly, one of her flock was attacked by a mountain lion. Yelling and throwing rocks, the Indian woman bravely fought off the lion while the rest of her goats panicked and ran in all directions.

When the lion was gone, the woman began rounding up her scattered herd. It was then that she stumbled upon a ledge containing an outcropping of gold.

Although she was excited by her find, the wise old woman kept the news to herself. Soon, however, she was making frequent trips to town (probably Monrovia), where she sold the precious rock. A jeweler is said to have purchased most of the gold to resell at a tidy profit.

Modern-day fortune hunters still prospect in the Fish Canyon area, and some claim to have found a considerable amount of gold. Such stories become more credible when we consider that, according to one source, the padres at Mission San Gabriel were also interested in the "yellow stuff." In fact, so interested were they that they sent Indians to the area to placer-mine the streams. How much gold they found is unknown, but the same source goes on to say that since the days of the padres over eight million dollars in gold has been taken from the San Gabriel River system!

Another account that involves Mission San Gabriel tells of Indians taking treasure *from* the church, rather than helping to bring it in. This story states that long ago, when the missions were prosperous, a group of Indians hid millions of dollars' worth of church valuables. Most treasure buffs discount the amount, since California's early churches were not in the habit of collecting vast sums of wealth. Nevertheless, rumors persisted that the bonanza was buried in the hills of nearby Monterey Park.

In the 1930s a treasure-seeking expedition is said to have visited the Coyote Pass area of the Monterey Park hills in search of the valuables. The man in charge of the fortune-hunting crew claimed to be guided by a spirit. Unfortunately, either the man or the spirit must have become confused, as the treasure was never found.

So as not to discourage future fortune hunters, I should mention at this point that the Monterey Park area also boasts a treasure that *was* found! In the late 1870s, two workers who were digging on the bank of a dry creek found a heavy box. Taking it home, they excitedly opened it. To their delight—and good fortune—the box contained assorted valuables, including Mexican pesos, Spanish doubloons, bags of gold dust, and beautiful jewelry! No one knows who buried the box. Although the finders wouldn't tell how much the treasure was worth, one source estimated its value at between $30,000 and $50,000!

All in all, a remarkable number of treasure tales are connected with the area around Mission San Gabriel. In ending this chapter, it seems only fitting to tell of a treasure that reportedly was found on the grounds of the mission itself.

The story states that in 1878 a quantity of gold coins was unearthed during the excavation of a grave. As you might guess, the find caused considerable concern—not to mention a "mini" gold rush to the church cemetery! Order was soon restored, however, and future treasure hunters chose to seek their fortunes in places other than Mission San Gabriel's historic graveyard.

Mission Santa Barbara

Mission Santa Barbara was the tenth mission to be established. It was founded in 1786 by Padre Fermin Francisco de Lasuen.

Mission Santa Barbara

Often called the Queen of the Missions, stately Mission Santa Barbara is one of the most frequently visited historical sites in California. Probably the first things that catch a visitor's eye are the church's magnificent twin bell towers—the only "twin towers" along the entire Mission Trail. But a closer look reveals many other fascinating features of this queenly church.

One of the mission's most striking features is its unique and imposing facade, which is bordered by the matching Spanish bell towers. Historians still argue whether the facade is Greek or Roman in design. Either way, it is an impressive reminder of the Old World heritage the Spanish brought to California.

Speaking of the Spanish, Santa Barbara is the only mission in the coastal chain that has remained under the influence of the Franciscans, Padre Serra's religious order, since its founding. Keeping vigil inside the beautiful church is a flickering altar light. Although not as old as the mission itself, the altar flame has been kept burning continuously for more than 150 years!

There is also a spookier relic of the past that is guaranteed to give visitors the goosebumps. If you get the chance to visit the church, look for the pair of human skulls that guard the door leading from the church to the cemetery.

Another feature that connects the present-day mission with days of long ago is its elaborate water system of dams, reservoirs, and aqueducts. Although the system was originally built by the padres and the Indians, part of it is still in use today, more than 200 years later!

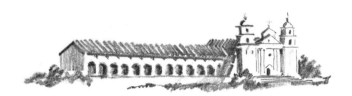

There are many unique things about Mission Santa Barbara, but for me its most fascinating aspect is the multitude of tales that are told about it—and about its surrounding areas.

Among the stories is an account of privateer Hippolyte de Bouchard. Considered a pirate by some, Bouchard sailed under the flag of the Republic of Buenos Aires. In 1818 this fiery Frenchman became the scourge of coastal California, among other things attacking and plundering the capital city of Monterey. (You will read more about this episode in the Carmel Mission chapter.)

At Santa Barbara, however, Bouchard may have been outwitted. The mission padres and the commander of the presidio staged a colossal bluff, convincing Bouchard that the settlement was protected by a much larger force than the Spanish really had. The two sides exchanged prisoners that had been taken before the privateer's arrival in Santa Barbara, and Bouchard continued down the California coast without mounting an attack.

Incidentally, as with other seaside communities, the residents of Santa Barbara had been forewarned of Bouchard's coming. Before heading inland to escape the wrath of this feared freebooter, many of the townsfolk hid their wealth in and about the places they lived.

One such stash—which included such prized valuables as silver candlesticks and glittering jewelry—was deposited at the bottom of a well. The rock-lined shaft was 60 feet deep and contained more than 20 feet of water at its base.

Unfortunately, when the owners of the property returned to their residence, no one could be found to venture down the well and dive for the treasure. Several attempts to snag the valuables and bring them to the surface proved fruitless.

As the years rolled on, the waterlogged treasure remained at the bottom of the shaft. Finally, time took its toll, and the well collapsed. Today the treasure remains buried. It will probably stay that way for some time, as a multilevel parking garage is built on top of it!

The treasure at the bottom of the well is not the only one associated with plunderers from the sea. On the outskirts of Santa Barbara, a pirate treasure is said to be stashed. The booty was hastily hidden by a band of buccaneers who were being pursued by a Mexican gunboat. Supposedly the treasure is still buried in the vicinity of the popular Arroyo Burro Beach Park.

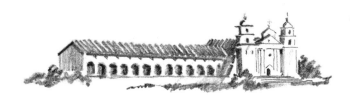

While on the subject of pirates, I can't help but think of other California badmen. With this in mind it is of interest to note that the famed bandit Joaquin Murrieta is also a part of local history. According to one report, in the 1880s a man obtained a map that showed where a portion of the fabled Murrieta loot was hidden. Coming to Santa Barbara, he dutifully followed the markings on the map—and was rewarded with a haul of valuables worth an estimated $14,000!

While it is interesting to speculate how much more bandit loot is stashed in the Santa Barbara area, a second story about Joaquin Murrieta is more to my liking. According to this account, in the early 1850s the daring desperado attended a fandango held under a huge grapevine near the mission. When the local sheriff learned that the notorious bandito was at the gathering, he set out to capture him. However, Murrieta was tipped off and made his escape. As he left, he broke a small branch from the grapevine, which he planted in a nearby ravine. Today, the story goes, that still-growing grapevine is over a mile in length!

A second tale about Santa Barbara's remarkable grapevine is intertwined with one of California's most romantic legends. The story concerns the lovely Concepcion Arguello, who remained faithful to a Russian count even after he tragically met his death in far-off Siberia. This devoted lady took charge of a school for young girls that was conducted under the management of the mission. According to the story, she once used a twig from the mission grapevine as a riding whip. One of her admirers, a devoted pupil, planted that very twig, and it grew to be one of the largest grapevines in the world.

For those who are more attracted by lost treasures than grapevines, the area around Santa Barbara has other riches to seek out. San Marcos Pass, for example, may be just the place to look. A quick check of a map will show that the pass crosses the Santa Ynez Mountains behind Santa Barbara. In days of old, before modern-day automobiles whizzed over the pass, travel was mostly by horse-drawn wagon and buggies. Stagecoaches also found their way over the rough mountain road. And it is the long-ago robbery of one of the stages that this account is about.

A lone bandit was to blame for the deed. According to the tale, he not only made off with a strongbox containing $30,000 in gold, but he robbed the occupants of the stage as well.

As the coach continued on its way, the highwayman buried the strongbox in a canyon near the top of the pass.

Supposedly the box is still there, for the culprit who committed the crime was killed before he could return to claim his prize.

Another treasure tale brings us back to the mission itself. According to an account that persists to this day, two Indians once brought a sack of gold ore to the church. When the padres saw what was in the sack, they feared that other Indians would forsake the mission to seek the source of the ore. Thinking quickly, they told the Indians that the gold was contaminated. Instructing them to tell no one of their discovery, the padres told the Indians to return the ore to the place where they had found it. As the Indians obediently retraced their steps, the padres tried to follow them. But their clever plan failed when they lost the track of the Indians, and the whereabouts of the gold remains a mystery.

A treasure story of more recent vintage tells of loot that was hidden by a solitary bandit of the 1920s. Called the Lone Wolf because he preferred to work by himself, this enterprising thief was quite successful even though he never carried a gun. Eventually, though, he was caught and sent to San Quentin Prison.

Before he could complete his jail term, the Lone Wolf became desperately ill. Knowing he would never be free again, the dying bandit met with the prison warden and told him that part of his loot was buried in a wild raspberry patch near west Santa Barbara. The stolen treasure is estimated to be worth more than $100,000, and supposedly it is still buried beneath the raspberries, waiting to be found.

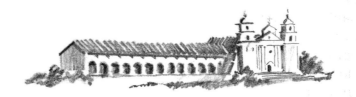

I could go on with more tales of treasure, but to me the most amazing story about the Santa Barbara area has nothing to do with pirates, outlaws, or gold. Instead, it concerns a remarkable and courageous Indian woman and a small island approximately 70 miles from the California shore.

To appreciate this tale we must go back to 1835. It was in this year that the padres at Mission Santa Barbara asked an American sea captain to visit the island of San Nicolas and bring the Indians who lived there to the mainland.

Despite being the most distant of California's offshore islands, San Nicolas originally supported a thriving Indian population. However, when the demand for sea otter skins brought hunters to their remote shores, the San Nicolans' way of life was drastically changed. With little regard for the people of the island, the fur hunters took what they wanted and often killed anyone who got in the way. Before long only about 25 Indians were left on the island.

This was the situation when the rescue vessel braved a Pacific storm and dropped anchor off the island shore. Once the Indians realized that the intruders were there to help rather than harm them, they accepted the offer of rescue and prepared to leave their island home.

As the Indians hastily packed their belongings, the storm became worse. By the time they were ready to board the small boats that would take them to the rescue ship, fierce winds were blowing, and giant swells threatened to swamp the boats. With great skill the sailors guided their craft to the waiting schooner, and everyone boarded safely.

It was then that tragedy struck. After reaching the deck of the ship, a young mother began searching frantically for her lost baby. Horrified, she learned it had been left behind! Upon pleading with the captain to return to San Nicolas, she was told that the sailors couldn't risk going back. To tempt the storm-wracked water any longer might mean destruction of the ship—perhaps even the death of everyone aboard.

Even though the captain indicated he would return the next day if the storm subsided, the distraught mother couldn't stand the thought of leaving her baby for even one night. Thinking of the wild dogs and other dangers lurking on the island, she lunged for the rail and threw herself into the Pacific.

On board the schooner, the other Indians and the crew were able to glimpse the young mother desperately swimming toward the island. Soon she was lost to sight. Even the best swimmer, they knew, would have little chance of reaching the island alive—and even then she was likely to be dashed against the rocks. Helpless and disheartened, all aboard the vessel could only pray that somehow she would survive.

With the storm blowing and great waves toying with his ship, the captain decided to head for the mainland with his precious human cargo. Hoping to return to San Nicolas in case the Indian woman had made it to the shore alive, the captain found other orders waiting for him instead. These orders eventually took him to San Francisco, where his vessel was lost as it neared the entrance of the bay.

Back in Santa Barbara, no other ships were available to attempt another rescue. As the days, weeks, and months passed by, the fate of the young mother was talked about less and less. Those who did discuss the incident thought she must have drowned. And if by some miracle she *had* reached the island, as time went on it seemed less and less likely that she or her baby could have survived the harsh conditions with no other human beings there to help them. Eventually the story of the brave young mother who risked her life to save her child was forgotten by all but a few.

Among those who did remember the tale were the padres at Mission Santa Barbara. But with no ship at their disposal, there was little they could do.

Fifteen long years went by. Then, one day, an otter-hunting expedition chanced to stop at the mission. During their visit, the otter hunters heard the story of the abandoned woman from the mission padres. Impressed by the tale, the visitors agreed to look for signs of what had happened to her if they managed to reach the island.

Upon arriving at San Nicolas, members of the ship's crew were surprised to find indications of someone having lived on the island after the Indian population had left. Seeing nothing to suggest that anyone was still there, they were considerably more excited by the abundance of seals and sea otters they found in the area. After their return to the mainland, however, their stories of what they had seen soon began to spread up and down the Santa Barbara shore.

The crew members' stories generated considerable excitement. Before long another expedition set out for San Nicolas to hunt the otters and seals—and to check more thoroughly for any hints that someone might be living there.

After setting up camp on the San Nicolas shore, some of the crew members attempted to search the island. However, once they saw the abundance of otters and seals on the beaches and in the nearby waters, their interest in the search waned. For more than a month the crew's energies were directed toward capturing and killing the helpless creatures. At last, having filled their vessel with skins, the seafarers prepared to leave the wind-swept island.

As the crew made ready to sail, a storm came up. Waves and wind pounded the ship, damaging one of the masts and parting the anchor chain. Frantically the men fixed the mast, but not before they were swept dangerously close to shore. Finally they gained the upper hand and gratefully pointed the ship toward the mainland.

It was then that one of the exhausted crew members happened to glance back at the island and the jagged rocks that jutted into the sea. The sailor blinked in disbelief. Above the rocks was the figure of a woman standing on a ridge!

The astonished sailor called to his shipmates. Rushing to his side, they strained to see the solitary figure through the wind-whipped spray of the raging sea. Soon the apparition was lost to sight.

Because only some of the crew had seen her, a number of stories began to circulate aboard the ship. Some said a wild woman was living all alone on the deserted island. Others whispered that the sailors had seen the image of a ghost!

Back on the island, the lone woman breathed a sigh of relief as she watched the sailors go—just as she had done when the first visitors had left. Hardly a ghost, and far from wild, she had kept herself hidden from view during the strangers' stays on the island. She remembered all too well how the otter hunters of long ago had treated her people, and she was afraid to let these new intruders know she was there. Now that they were gone, she no longer had to worry. She was free to roam the island openly, alone once again with the animals and birds.

When the seafarers reached the Santa Barbara shore, the mission padres and others who heard their tale insisted that another trip be made. As incredible as it seemed, the solitary woman of San Nicolas must be the young mother who had been left behind so many years before!

This third voyage in as many years finally solved the mystery of San Nicolas. This time the woman was found, and her rescuers managed to persuade her that they only wanted to help her. With a last look at her island home, she boarded the vessel and set sail for the mainland.

Gradually the remarkable story of the island woman came to light. After jumping ship 18 years before, she had made it to the island and searched desperately for her lost child. Sadly, the baby was nowhere to be found. Despite her heartbreak, the young mother realized that the ship was not about to turn back. Somehow she had to find a way to survive all alone.

Fortunately, she remembered the lessons she had learned growing up. With practice and hard work she obtained food, built shelters, and made clothing, including a shiny robe she fashioned entirely from cormorant feathers.

Weeks turned into months, and months into years, and still no ship called at San Nicolas. In time the woman adapted to her lonely life, building huts and hideaways in various parts of the island. Remembering how cruelly the otter hunters had treated her people, she hid these shelters in case the hunters returned.

One day, when she was walking about the island, she found two puppies whose mother had died. Even though their mother had been part of a pack of wild dogs that roamed the island, the pups responded to the woman's kindness and began to follow her about. Soon a great friendship developed between them. After years of being completely alone, the island woman had two trusted companions to keep her company.

The solitary queen of a deserted island, for almost 20 years she did not speak to another human being.

Needless to say, the people on the mainland marveled when they heard the woman's amazing story of courage and perseverance. Upon arriving at Santa Barbara, she was warmly welcomed by the padres and the residents of the coastal town. Treated with admiration and respect, she was showered with gifts, many of which she kindly gave to local children.

Unfortunately, even though she was happy and cared for in Santa Barbara, soon after her rescue she became ill. Despite the best efforts of the townspeople, the woman who had survived all alone on a rugged island steadily weakened, until at last the sickness took her life.

Before she died she was given the name Juana Maria by her new friends. Today her memory lives on in the cemetery of Mission Santa Barbara, where a plaque on the wall commemorates her remarkable story. If you happen to visit the Queen of the Missions, I hope you will seek out the plaque and join me in saluting Juana Maria, the brave and lonely queen of the island of San Nicolas.

Mission San Antonio

Mission San Antonio de Padua was the third mission to be established. It was founded in 1771 by Padre Junipero Serra.

Mission
San Antonio

Mission San Antonio is often described as the most remote of California's coastal missions. One of the few missions to remain in a rural setting, the aged church retains a feeling of timelessness and mystery.

In fact, the San Antonio area is full of mysteries, including one tale that goes all the way back to the mission's earliest days. It seems that not long after the mission's founding, an aged Indian woman (said to be nearly 100 years old) came to the padres asking to be baptized. When the delighted church fathers asked why she desired baptism, she told them a story she had heard from her parents as a child. According to the story, another man dressed like the padres had come to the Valley of the Oaks long ago. The stranger had told the same stories of the cross that the padres were telling. It was the memory of her parent's tales of this man and his stories that had prompted her to come to the mission.

Mystified, the padres proceeded to question the old woman further about the long-ago visitor. In response she told how the "other" padre had not come by land. Instead, on four different occasions, he had come to her ancestors through the air!

Amazed and baffled by the woman's account, the mission padres asked other local Indians whether they had heard similar tales. To their surprise, the majority of those who lived in the valley knew about the "flying padre." Furthermore, the mission fathers learned that the story was handed down from generation to generation as part of the lore of the local Indians.

What explanation can we give for the Indian legend? As far as anyone knows, no priests had visited the San Antonio Valley before Spain began colonizing Alta California. However, a similar account from nearly a thousand miles away may shed some light on the intriguing story.

According to this tale, about 150 years before Serra began his chain of coastal missions, a tribe of Indians in the American Southwest (probably present-day New Mexico) sent messengers to some distant padres, asking for missionaries to come to their land and baptize them. This request astonished the padres. How had the Indians heard of baptism? The mystery only deepened when the padres reached the Indians' homeland. To their amazement, the New Mexico Indians were so well-informed about the padres' religion that they were ready to be baptized without further instruction!

While many people have dismissed this episode as a legend, others have probed further, hoping to find evidence of some earlier missionary who had visited the Indians of New Mexico. Their efforts uncovered still another strange tale, this one from far-off Spain. According to an aged document, there once was a Spanish nun who was said to have miraculous powers. This devoted nun, the document went on to say, had flown to the Indians of the Southwest and shared her beliefs with them. In telling of her adventures, she had even described the Indian lands she had visited and events that had taken place there.

What do these stories of happenings in New Mexico and Spain have to do with the Indians of the San Antonio Valley? Well, one source claims that the valley's Indians resembled the New Mexico natives in important ways. For instance, in preparing their food the San Antonio Indians are described as having used the traditional southwestern *manos* and *metates* (rubbing and grinding stones), rather than the mortars and pestles that were more common in other parts of California. Even more significant, the language of the valley's Indians is said to resemble that of a group of Indians in New Mexico.

With these thoughts in mind, some researchers wonder whether the San Antonio Indians might originally have drifted to the valley from the Southwest, bringing with them the New Mexico legend of an airborne missionary.

Another theory suggests that a priest from some other New World outpost may have ventured into the San Antonio area before Serra's arrival and taught the Indians the story of the cross. Perhaps this forgotten padre even mentioned the legend of the flying nun. If so, the stories may have become intertwined over the years, so that later generations of Indians believed that it was *he* who had come to them through the sky.

Whatever the answer is, the Indians of this beautiful valley have presented history buffs with a fascinating puzzle—one that only adds to the mystique of the valley and its secluded church.

A more down-to-earth mystery that revolves around Mission San Antonio concerns the disappearance of a sizable treasure—$50,000 in gold! In telling this tale, I should mention that the churches along the El Camino Real were not in the habit of collecting large sums of money. San Antonio's unusual accumulation of wealth is credited to the sale of the fine horses that were raised at the mission. People from throughout California were willing to pay handsome prices for the outstanding mounts, which were prized for their speed, strength, beauty, and courage.

As for the treasure, in the early 1800s a small group of Indians and a lone soldier are said to have set out from the mission. The Indians were burdened with packs of coins that were destined for a vessel anchored in a small harbor on the west side of the coastal mountains. The ship was to transport the gold to a port in Mexico. There it was to be transferred to the church treasury in Mexico City.

Unfortunately, somewhere between the mission and the harbor, the Indians, the soldier, and the money disappeared! Tellers of this tale say that robbers ambushed the party and made off with the gold. Interestingly, a second tale tells of weekend gold seekers who claim to have found old Spanish coins along a stream in the Santa Lucia Mountains. Known as Willow Creek, it was this stream that the Indians and their lone guard were supposed to have followed on their way to the coast.

While it is at least possible that parts of the lost treasure have been found, I can't help but wonder what became of the Indians and the soldier. For those who knew the story, considerable excitement was created more than 150 years after their disappearance, in 1962. It was in that year that four prospectors from the San Francisco Bay Area made a startling discovery—one that, at first, seemed to solve the mystery.

One August afternoon, the modern-day gold seekers saw bats darting in and out of a small opening on a Santa Lucia cliff. Curious about the crevice the creatures called home, the foursome carefully made their way up the cliff.

Perhaps it was tales of the famed Lost Padre Mine (or mines) that aroused their curiosity, or maybe it was the numerous accounts of gold in the Santa Lucia Mountains that spurred them on. Whatever the case, by the time they reached the opening, their imaginations had taken charge, and they were anxious to see what might be found in the crevice besides bats!

After some serious digging, the prospectors discovered that the opening was an entrance to a much larger cave. With fingers crossed and hopes high, they squeezed into the chamber—and froze in their tracks. Scattered on the cave floor was an assortment of human bones!

After a quick inspection the explorers realized that the bones had been in the cave for a very long time. They also discovered that the main floor of the chamber dropped to a second level, and then a third. Further exploration at a later date disclosed that there were bones on all three levels.

The gold seekers notified authorities of their grisly find, and before long a group of county sheriffs arrived on the scene, along with members of the local press. While various explanations of the bones were proposed, it was generally agreed that human beings had not used the cave for a living site. Later, an anthropologist examined the bones and concluded that most of them were the remains of Indians. However, he also said that one of the skulls was probably European rather than Indian, and possibly came from a Spaniard!

When this information was made public, those who were familiar with the disappearance of the Spanish soldier and the band of Indians were confident that the mystery had been solved. However, later information indicated that the bones had lain in the cave for only about 100 years, too short a time to link them with the lost mission treasure.

As so often happens in history, the pieces of the puzzle didn't quite fit. Instead, one mystery had led to another. Today history buffs still speculate about the origins of the bones. As for the soldier and the Indians—not to mention the $50,000 in gold—whatever might be left of them remains to be found.

The topic of gold in the Santa Lucias, mentioned in the preceding account, brings us back to the San Antonio side of the mountains.

If you looked at a detailed map of southern Monterey County, you would see two small canyons with the same intriguing name—China Gulch. One lies in a northwesterly direction from the mission, and the other in a southwesterly direction. Old-timers say the canyons' names date back to the mid-1800s, when drifters from California's famed Gold Country (in the Sierra Nevada) were trying their luck in the foothills of the Santa Lucias. Some of these gold seekers had originally come from China. Sadly, a number of the Chinese had been roughly treated in the Sierras. Chased from their diggings, they drifted to other parts of California.

Some of those who found their way to central California must have looked longingly at the Santa Lucias, wondering whether there was gold to be found in the rugged coastal mountains. Perhaps they even heard stories of lost padre mines and tales of Indian wealth that fired their imaginations. Whatever it was that ignited the spark, Chinese gold seekers were soon searching for the elusive yellow metal in the gullies and streams of the San Antonio area. And so it was that two of the areas being worked by the Chinese both came to be known as China Gulch.

To the surprise of many, it was not long before the Chinese found what they were looking for. Other canyons, such as Mission Creek and Oro Fino (Fine Gold) Canyon also yielded the precious metal. As word of the finds spread, prospectors from afar decided to have a look.

Soon the nearby mountains were filled with seekers of fortune, and claims were staked throughout much of the territory. By 1875 things were getting out of hand, and the Los Burros Mining District was formed to help organize the area and keep order. Twelve years later, the area's best-paying mine was discovered. Known as the Last Chance Mine, it produced a considerable amount of gold . . . and also added to the area's tales of mystery.

The first such tale took place in 1907, when a man named William T. Cruikshank set out for San Francisco. Cruikshank was the Los Burros District's first recorder of claims and the father of the man who founded the Last Chance Mine. When last seen hiking out of the area, the elder Cruikshank appeared to be healthy and making good progress. However, he was never seen again—dead or alive!

Mystery number two took place 30 years later and involves Cruikshank's son, who was also named William. Strangely enough, he, too, disappeared while hiking out of Los Burros! Ten years later, his bones were found by soldiers on military maneuvers. Amazingly, still clasped to his wrist was a silver watch with initials engraved on it. The initials were those of his mining partner, the man he was on his way to see. (The partner lived in King City, approximately 18 miles from Mission San Antonio.) Interestingly, it was this man—then in his eighties—who told me the story. Today the circumstances surrounding the disappearances of the two mining pioneers remain unknown, but the oddly similar fates of father and son add a strange puzzle to the area's collection of local lore.

Another intriguing tale that is connected with the San Antonio area has puzzled historians for many years. The mystery concerns the significance of drawings found on the walls of an ancient Indian cave. Rock art such as this is relatively rare in this part of California, and those who have studied the illustrations think that the oldest ones may date back as much as a thousand years!

Identified by some as ceremonial in nature, the drawings include an interesting assortment of shapes and designs. At the heart of the puzzle are some designs in the shapes of large and small crosses, similar to Christian symbols. Some sources indicate that the crosses were drawn on the cave walls long before the mission was built and were seen by the area's earliest padres, including Father Serra.

If this account is accurate, one can't help but wonder why Indians would draw crosses before they had heard about Christianity from the padres. Could there be some connection with the tale of an earlier padre who came to the Indians through the air? Whatever the explanation, the crosses in the cave add yet another puzzle to our ever-growing list of San Antonio mysteries.

Puzzles continue to crop up the more we look into the history of the Valley of the Oaks. Having discussed crosses in the previous account, I am reminded of a second story about just such a symbol. This tale takes place at the mission in the late 1800s. Much of the mission had fallen into ruin by this time, but the crumbling buildings still attracted their share of visitors. Among those who were present when this incident took place were a group of local residents who had gathered for a picnic.

Finding a small clearing in the high dry grass near the aged church, the small party of picnickers settled down for an enjoyable summer outing. Suddenly they heard the sounds of an approaching rider. Standing to see who the newcomer might be, the picnickers were surprised to see a lone cowboy pull his horse to a stop in front of the mission.

Not knowing who he was, or what he was doing there, the picnickers watched as the cowboy took his rope and lassoed the cross on the building's roof. The cross was already leaning at an angle from age and neglect, and it was obvious to the onlookers that it couldn't withstand the pull of the rope for long. As the cowboy wound his lasso around his saddle horn and started to back away, the picnickers ran toward the church, shouting for him to stop.

Losing sight of the stranger as they ran through the grass, the picnickers were forced to come to a sudden stop as the cowboy's riderless horse galloped past them. Confused about what had happened, and concerned about the rider, the picnickers began a frantic search of the area. Soon they found the stranger's lifeless body in the brush.

To this day old-timers who are familiar with the tale are at a loss to explain how the cowboy died . . . but they do know that the cross he had tried to pull down remained in its place atop the mission.

Many more riddles and interesting anecdotes are told about the San Antonio area. One story tells of a cloud that appeared in the courtyard of the church and followed the path that used to be walked by a priest who had recently died. Other spooky accounts include sightings of mysterious lights in the area around the mission and legends of a headless woman on horseback who has been observed by old-timers (and some not so old). Less supernatural are reports of a fossilized whale that juts from a canyon wall and the odd tale of a singing cricket that lived in the crack of a small boy's foot (causing him to carry his shoes rather than wear them). Treasure tales abound, too, including one that tells of the discovery of a secret tunnel at Los Burros that headed straight for the shaft of the Last Chance Mine.

Among the area's enduring secrets are the locations of two treasure sites. One is a lost silver mine (known as the Priest Mine) that the church fathers were said to have worked. The other is a hidden pasture—complete with cave—where California badman Tiburcio Vasquez hid his stolen mounts . . . and his loot!

As for "found" treasure, I'm sure seekers of fortune would like to know the contents of a mysterious metal box that was dug from the floor of a back room at Mission San Antonio itself. If it was money, most agree, it was probably spent long ago, as this story dates back to the late 1800s.

With so many local stories centering on mystery and lost riches, it's only fitting to end this chapter with a final tale of treasure and intrigue. According to this account, not far from the mission a considerable cache of riches may be concealed.

This rare treasure is said to date back hundreds of years—perhaps to the days of the Aztecs! The Aztec Indians occupied much of what we now know as Mexico. Described as one of the most civilized and powerful groups of ancient America, the Aztecs came to power in about 1200 and ruled a mighty empire until they were conquered by the Spanish in 1521.

Before the Spanish conquest, legend states, the Aztec emperor Montezuma instructed some of his most trusted followers to take portions of the vast Aztec wealth to a number of distant locations for safekeeping. Upon reaching their destinations and concealing the riches in caves and chambers, the leaders of the expedition are said to have killed the slaves who carried the valuables. They then sealed the slaves' bodies in the treasure tombs.

After the Spanish conquest and the death of Montezuma, stories began to circulate about secret caches of Aztec wealth. Many of the accounts are little more than rumor and legends that have been added to over the years. However, in the 1960s an event occurred in the San Antonio area that makes one think twice about such tales.

Supposedly this story got its start in a monastery in far-off Canada. After much research, a professional treasure hunter had located and sketched an aged Indian map that was kept in the monastery. The map led him to a spot in the foothills of the Santa Lucias where he thought a great Aztec treasure was stashed. Unfortunately, the site was on government-owned land within the military post that today surrounds Mission San Antonio.

This discovery put a damper on things, since the treasure hunter knew it would be difficult to get permission to excavate the site, or to keep whatever he found there. Even so, he did explore the area a bit and managed to drill a hole where he thought a tunnel led to the treasure trove. When his drilling revealed a cavity (opening) beneath the ground, he was all the more confident he had found the right site.

As promising as this initial work was, the fellow who found the map realized that his hopes of laying claim to fantastic riches would be dashed if he had to surrender the treasure to the government. Soon he abandoned his dream and left the area.

Today the tunnel—if that is what the man found—remains unexplored. What lies at the tunnel's end? Is there really a hoard of Indian treasure waiting to be found? As with so many stories of the area around Mission San Antonio, the answers are a mystery. But in this case I'm willing to make a prediction—and that is, we haven't heard the last of this treasure tale yet!

Mission San Carlos

(Carmel Mission)

Mission San Carlos Borromeo del Rio Carmelo was the second mission to be established. It was founded in 1770 by Padre Junipero Serra.

Mission
San Carlos
(Carmel Mission)

The church known to most people today as Carmel Mission was the second church to be established by Padre Junipero Serra. Founded in 1770, it is officially known as Mission San Carlos Borromeo del Rio Carmelo (the Mission of St. Charles Borromeo of the Carmel River). It was this mission that Padre Serra made his home, and it was here that he died and was buried.

As you might expect of the church that became the hub of California's mission movement, Carmel Mission's history is rich in fascinating stories. One of my favorites concerns an incident that took place even before the church got its start.

To appreciate this tale we must go back to 1769, and Gaspar de Portola's unsuccessful attempt to find Monterey Bay. Basing his search on a chronicle kept by explorer Sebastian Vizcaino in 1602, Portola unknowingly led his men to the shores of the bay. Unfortunately, he failed to recognize the wind-swept inlet as the calm and secure harbor Vizcaino had described. Making camp on the south side of the Monterey Peninsula (in the vicinity of the present Carmel church), Portola and his men continued their search for the elusive bay of Monterey.

Finally, still not realizing he was only a short hike from the inlet he was so desperately seeking, the disappointed Portola decided to return to San Diego. Before departing, he erected two crosses to commemorate the expedition, complete with messages to seafarers telling of the Spaniards' problems and their lack of success. One cross was placed on the shore of Carmel Bay, and the other on the beach of the very bay they were seeking.

Following the long and difficult return trip to San Diego, Portola met with Father Serra. After reviewing the Vizcaino chronicle, they realized that Portola had in fact found Monterey Bay. With the arrival of the long-awaited supply ship (as related in the Mission San Diego chapter), Portola and Serra were able to continue their efforts to establish new outposts in Alta California. Eagerly they made plans for a second expedition to Monterey.

On this second trip Serra was to seek Monterey Bay by sea, while Portola again made the difficult trek by land. All went according to plan, and the Spaniards had a joyful reunion on the Monterey shore. Standing in the shade of a mighty oak, Serra led the company in prayers of thanksgiving, and ceremonies were held to mark the official founding of Monterey, its accompanying presidio, and Mission San Carlos Borromeo. This historic event took place on June 3, 1770—about six years before the signing of the Declaration of Independence gave birth to a new nation on the other side of the American continent.

While the founding of California's first capital city opened a new chapter in the history of the Golden State, the tale I started to tell involves a curious episode that was connected with this event. As you recall, on his first trip north Portola had left a cross on the shores of Monterey Bay. When the second expedition returned to the site, they were in for quite a surprise! The cross was still standing on the lonely beach, but now it was accompanied by a variety of objects. The collection included several arrows arranged in a circle and pointing to the cross, a cluster of feathers (thought to be from an eagle), a string of fresh fish, and a neat mound of mussels.

The Spaniards were mystified by the decorations. What could their meaning be? It wasn't until some time later that local Indians told the padres what had occurred. During the night, they said, the cross had seemed to glow with light and to reach far up into the heavens! Awed by this event, the Indians had brought peace offerings to the visitors' god.

In recalling the Indians who may have witnessed the spectacle of the glowing cross, I can't help but think of one Indian who saw a lot of history being made during his long life. Known as Old Gabriel, by some accounts he was already a grandfather when Padre Serra arrived on the scene. If so, he must have been hale and hearty for his age, for tradition states that he helped to build the original Carmel church, as well as the more permanent structure that replaced it later on. And from there he went on to take part in the construction of two more missions, those at Soledad and San Antonio.

A legend in his own time, Gabriel was said to have been so nimble in his youth that he could dodge arrows shot directly at him. Remaining strong and full of vitality as he grew older, he outlived six or seven wives and fathered many children. One of his sons supposedly lived to be more than 100—but Old Gabriel outlived him, too!

Needless to say, as the years went on the padres were more and more amazed by Old Gabriel. One priest in nearby Salinas first met Gabriel when the Indian was already an old man. Thirty-six years later, with Gabriel still alive and well, the priest decided to share the remarkable story with the church fathers in far-off Italy. As proof of the tale, he sent a picture of the ancient Indian to Rome, along with documents from old-timers stating that Gabriel was already old when they were young. This brought the aged California native considerable fame, as his portrait hung for a time in the church buildings at the Vatican, along with information indicating that he was the oldest man in the world!

Just how old was Gabriel when he died? We may never know for certain. Although his tombstone at Carmel Mission indicates that he lived to the astonishing age of 151, additional research has cast doubt on this figure. Today a more recent plaque states that he was "only" 119 at the time of his death.

The subject of graves at Carmel Mission brings to mind an individual who earned his fame in a very different way— an early California badman by the name of Anastacio Garcia. It was Garcia who taught the outlaw trade to the even more notorious Tiburcio Vasquez (whom we met in the chapter on Mission San Gabriel). Among Garcia's other "claims to fame" is the killing of several people, including five victims connected with a well-known treasure feud. (Incidentally, there are rumors that the treasure—known as the Sanchez treasure, and said to consist of $85,000 in gold—remains hidden in the area, perhaps between Monterey and Carmel Mission.)

Eventually Garcia was captured and brought to Monterey, where a group of local men intent on hanging him broke into his cell. According to a local legend, before being strung up Garcia asked to be buried "where the worshippers of the mission might ever tread upon his grave." And to this day, tradition states, his unmarked grave lies near the entrance of the Carmel church.

There are also many stories connecting the Monterey and Carmel areas with the most notorious California badman of all, Joaquin Murrieta. To history buffs familiar with the story of the Golden State, Murrieta is as famous an outlaw as Jesse James and Billy the Kid. Even though he committed most of his crimes in California's Gold Country, he is also suspected of terrorizing many other parts of the state. With a price on his head and the California Rangers hot on his trail, this Mother Lode marauder hid out in a variety of locations. At one point, while he was eluding a posse from the Santa Clara Valley, he apparently was given shelter at Carmel Mission itself. As the story goes, a young priest not only hid the desperado from the posse but also painted the only true likeness of him that is known to exist.

Imagining Joaquin Murrieta being holed up in the Carmel church, it's natural to wonder whether bandit treasure might be buried somewhere nearby. A number of stories of such hidden loot are told by local old-timers and reported in aged documents. Among them is one account of $75,000 worth of gold bars stolen from a mint in the Auburn area of the Gold Country. Several sources report rumors that Murrieta stashed the bars somewhere in or around the mission. In fact, one old newspaper account even states that about $10,000 worth of the gold was eventually recovered in the area.

Perhaps even more intriguing are accounts of a secret tunnel connecting the church to a neighboring area known as Mission Ranch. Numerous tales are told about this mysterious passageway. Some hint that it was here that Murrieta stashed his stolen gold. Other stories have suggested that the tunnel was part of a silver mine. (Interestingly, some pioneer residents claim that the church fathers once operated a rich silver mine in the area.) Still others propose that the passageway was meant to be an escape route for the padres in the event of an Indian uprising. And, lastly, there are those who wonder whether the tunnel led to a secret chamber where the church valuables were stored for safekeeping.

Speaking of church valuables, another interesting account of lost church treasure goes back to the year 1818, when Hippolyte de Bouchard brought fear and destruction to California's capital city. As related in the Santa Barbara chapter, Bouchard was a privateer who sailed under the flag of the Republic of Buenos Aires. Unlike Santa Barbara, Monterey was not spared from the fury of this adventurer of the high seas. After attacking and capturing the city, Bouchard and his men proceeded to take what they wanted and destroy much of what was left. For several days they plundered the helpless community, capturing livestock, robbing stores, destroying orchards, and burning buildings.

When the padres at Carmel Mission learned what was taking place on the opposite side of the hill, they were naturally concerned about what might happen to their church and its valuables. According to a local legend, the padres hurriedly gathered the most valued of the church artifacts and put them in a deerskin sack. Next they chose a trusted Indian—a man who happened to be blind—to carry the sack on his back to a hiding place in the foothills of the Santa Lucias.

After several detours down seldom-used paths, the odd little procession came to a great oak tree on a flat. It was here, under the spreading branches of the tree, that the padres decided to bury the valuables. With the cache carefully concealed, the padres led the blind Indian back to the mission.

Fortunately for the mission, Bouchard and his band of buccaneers had their fill of plunder and sailed out of Monterey Bay without so much as visiting the Carmel church. Once the danger had passed, the padres decided to fetch their valuables. Heading toward the coastal mountains, they soon realized they had neglected to mark the trail to the hiding place. Frantically they dug holes beneath the branches of one familiar-looking oak tree after another. At last they had to admit that their precious valuables were lost.

In looking back, it seems that the clever padres had outwitted themselves in choosing a blind helper to carry the treasure. With the Indians' skill and knowledge of the countryside, a helper who could see would surely have been able to lead them to their treasured artifacts.

The story of the too-clever padres is only one account of missing valuables connected with the missions. Even more plentiful are tales of lost gold and silver mines, especially the fabled "Lost Padre Mines" that were said to be located in the coastal mountains. The exact number of these mines is open to question. It seems that the more you look into these stories, the more Lost Padre Mines you can come up with. (Treasure buffs may wish to note that many of the missions are said to have had one or more such mines.)

In addition to Carmel's Lost Padre Mines, tales are also told about the mission's Lost Ventana Mine. According to one account, this cave of gold is about a day's walking distance from the church. More important, the mine is said to be in a direct southeasterly direction from a white scar on a large foothill of the nearby Santa Lucias.

The cliffside scar, which can easily be seen from the mission to this day, is the remains of a quarry where stones were obtained for use in the building of the church. The Indians who helped with the mission construction would chip the stones from their birdlike perch on the cliff and let them tumble down the steep hillside to the valley below. From there the stones were transported to the church.

As I indicated a moment ago, the Ventana Mine was supposed to be located somewhere southeast of the quarry. Its name—"ventana" is Spanish for "window"—fits nicely into the tale, because it provides a clue to the mine's location. Supposedly, someone standing at the entrance to the nugget-filled cave could see the bell tower of the mission. Not wanting the mine's location to become known, the church fathers swore the mission Indians to secrecy. But as so often happens with a story of gold, the secret leaked out . . . and ever since treasure seekers have been searching for the "lost window" of the Santa Lucias.

A second tale about Carmel Mission's Lost Ventana Mine gives a different account of the mine's name. According to this story, the name was taken from a tall mountain approximately 21 air miles from the church. Because of its two summits, the mountain is known as Ventana Double Cone. This story says that the peak acquired the name "Ventana" when early explorers noticed a ledge near its top that formed a small slot, or window.

Located in a southerly direction from the church, Ventana Double Cone is one of the highest mountains of the coastal range. Continuing in a southerly direction from this lofty peak, the story continues, a day's walk brought the Indians to a mountain that contained a shaft sprinkled with gold. Interestingly, also in a southerly direction from Ventana Double Cone is the Los Burros Mining District, where a considerable amount of gold has been found over the years. (The Los Burros Mining District was introduced in the Mission San Antonio chapter.) Even though Los Burros is more than a day's hike from Ventana Double Cone, this coincidence makes me wonder whether there is a grain of truth to this account of the Lost Ventana Mine.

There are many other stories about Indian gold in the Santa Lucias. One of my favorites tells about a mine located in a remote area known as Lost Valley (maybe it's this intriguing name that has captured my imagination). As the story goes, during the days of California's Mission Period, Spanish soldiers stumbled across the mine after tracking unsuspecting Indians to the site. Upon realizing what they had found, the greedy soldiers wasted little time in forcing the Indians to work the mine, while they pocketed the profits.

As time went on, the soldiers collected a considerable quantity of gold. But eventually the day came when the Indian workers turned on them. In the fight that followed, the Indians did away with their foe. From then on the whereabouts of the mine became a closely guarded secret.

Whether this story is true, I can't say. But reports do tell of Spanish coins, swords, and breastplates—along with a scattering of human bones—being found in the Lost Valley area. With this in mind, I can't help but wonder whether the old mine might be uncovered someday. If that happens, the Santa Lucias' Lost Valley might need a new name, since it will most certainly be "found" by many a modern-day gold seeker!

Closer to Carmel Mission, an area known as Point Lobos Reserve boasts one of California's most unusual tales of lost Indian gold. Supposedly the hidden wealth was located in a cave that could be entered only at certain times of the year. The rest of the time the cave was covered by water—not by just an ordinary pond, mind you, but by the mighty Pacific Ocean!

As you probably know, the world's oceans rise and fall with the tides caused by the gravitational pull of the sun and moon. Sometimes these tides are exceptionally high, and sometimes they are exceptionally low. It was at times of extremely low tides that the entrance of the cavern was exposed.

The Point Lobos cave, complete with its rich vein of gold, was on the face of a sheer cliff that dropped into a turbulent white water cove. Inside this underwater world, the constant churning of the Pacific washed bits of gold from the cavern's wall. When the tides were low enough, Indians gained access to the secret chamber by lowering themselves down the cliff with a cord-like rope they had patiently woven. After sidestepping the slippery seaweed and any sea creatures that had made their homes in the cave, the Indians could simply pick up the nuggets that were scattered about the floor.

As it happens, I once had the chance to discuss this hidden chamber with an elderly Monterey man who claimed to have ventured into it as a boy. When I brought up the subject of gold, he laughed and said, "The only 'color' I found in the cave was the red and black abalone [a type of shellfish] that clung to its ceiling and walls." Perhaps there is more truth to this comment than there is to the old legend of nuggets for the taking . . . but old treasure buffs like me can't help but wonder whether he was telling the whole story.

Unfortunately, the cave entrance collapsed in the 1940s, and from all indications Mother Nature did a remarkable job of sealing off the Indians' grotto of gold.

Certainly there is more truth than legend to many of the other tales that are told about the Point Lobos area.

Among these accounts are stories of whaling, shipwrecks, smuggling, coal mining, rock quarrying, abalone canning . . . and treasure hunting. One tale that may date back to the days of whaling in the 1860s tells about a long-lost treasure that (for once) was actually found—and then promptly lost again!

Appropriately enough, the story of the twice-lost treasure begins at Carmel Mission. In 1932 three treasure seekers from San Francisco visited the church. While camping on the grounds, they made many interesting discoveries with the aid of a homemade metal detector.

After tiring of prospecting near the mission, the men decided to try their luck at Point Lobos. Late one evening, they were crossing a flat near an old, weather-beaten whaler's cabin when their detector recorded a reading of buried metal! Knowing they were in an area that abounded in stories of lost wealth, the fortune hunters couldn't wait to begin digging. Unfortunately, a heavy Pacific fog had engulfed the point, and the evening darkness was beginning to fall. The men were rapidly getting cold and damp, and they were already exhausted from a long day of searching.

Talking all this over, the weary treasure seekers agreed whatever was buried had probably been there for many years and would still be there the next day. With such thoughts in mind they reluctantly decided to wait until morning to uncover their find.

As dawn broke the next day, the treasure seekers threw their digging tools into their car and headed eagerly for Point Lobos. When they reached the flat near the aged whaler's cabin, they jumped out of the car—and got the shock of their lives. At the exact spot they planned to dig was a freshly dug hole! And that wasn't all. At the bottom of the hole was the rusted imprint of a metal chest!

What was in the chest? Who dug it up? No one knows the answers to these questions except for whoever uncovered it. Probably the best guess is that the treasure was the savings of one of the 19th-century Portuguese whalers who plied their trade in the Point Lobos area. Certainly, many people in those long-ago days buried their valuables for safekeeping. Unfortunately, the only person or persons who could resolve the mystery may no longer be alive to tell what was found back in the 1930s—even supposing they wanted to talk!

Coincidentally, there is another story involving the rusted imprint of a metal container found at the bottom of a hole—this time in the Mission Ranch complex that borders Carmel Mission. This account tells of a hired hand who quit work early one afternoon. Bringing in the plow animals, he complained of not feeling well. Sympathizing with the man, the ranch foreman told him to put up the horses and take the rest of the afternoon off.

When the worker failed to arrive the following morning, the foreman hitched up the team and proceeded with plans to complete the plowing himself. Upon reaching the spot where the plow had been left, the foreman suddenly realized why his hired hand had not reported for work. Only a few feet from the blade of the plow was a neatly dug hole. At the base of the hole the foreman could see the imprint of a large iron pot.

Neither the pot nor its contents could be found. But with old rumors circulating that a container of gold coins had once been buried on the ranch, it didn't take the foreman long to diagnose his helper's "illness." A sickness that had previously infected many other Californians, it was known to old-timers as gold fever!

In ending this Carmel Mission chapter, another brief account about lost Indian gold seems appropriate. In reality this is two tales in one, as it tells about a pair of caves, each of which contained quills of gold!

Both caves are said to have been in the vicinity of the church, and both boasted ledges that had been carved into their walls. On the ledges were rows of bird feathers (thought to have been from seagulls). Inside the hollows of these feathers the Indians had tamped tiny particles of gold and an abundance of gold dust.

Why was gold placed in the hollows of bird feathers? No one seems to know. Some suggest it was just a novel way of storing the precious metal, while others claim it was an attempt by the Indians to fool their enemies. Perhaps they thought no one would think to look into the hollow of a bird feather for a valuable treasure. (Interestingly, other California Indians, as well as miners in New Mexico, were also in the habit of using the hollows of bird feathers to store their gold.)

Although both caves were close to the mission, they were in different directions. One is said to have been at the base of a rolling hill near a lagoon at the mouth of Carmel River. The other was located in a deep ravine, halfway up a steep cliff a few hundred yards north of the church.

Needless to say, these "Lost Caves of the Golden Quills" were stripped of their wealth long ago. Since then, wind, rain, and erosion have concealed their entrances, putting the seal of time on two more intriguing secrets of the past.

Mission Santa Clara

Mission Santa Clara de Asis was the eighth mission to be established. It was founded in 1777 by Padre Tomas de la Pena (under the guidance of Padre Junipero Serra).

Mission Santa Clara

Long ago, in the little-known Italian village of Assisi, two remarkable individuals made a quiet mark on history. The first is known today as Saint Francis. Famous for his gentle ways and his love of nature, it was Francis who founded the order of Franciscans, a band of religious men who devoted themselves to a simple life of prayer and preaching. The second was a pious woman named Clare, who was inspired by Francis to join the similar order he started for women. Like Francis, Clare was honored by her church after her death as a saint, and her order of nuns came to be known as the Poor Clares.

For centuries afterward, other dedicated men and women followed in the footsteps of the two Italian saints. Among them were the Spanish Franciscans, led by Padre Junipero Serra, who founded California's mission chain.

As you will learn in the next chapter, when the Spanish built their sixth mission in Alta California, they named it after the padres' beloved Saint Francis. Less than a year later, the eighth mission in the chain was established approximately 40 miles to the south. Appropriately enough, this new church was named in honor of Saint Clare.

In time, thriving communities grew up around both of these sites. And so it is that today, more than 700 years after their deaths, the memory of the gentle saints of Assisi lives on in the names of two bustling northern California cities—San Francisco and Santa Clara.

Like so many of the Alta California churches, Mission Santa Clara de Asis experienced a variety of hardships over the years. Floods, earthquakes, and fires all too often took their toll. Because of problems such as these, the mission changed locations more than any of its sister churches and was rebuilt several times.

The most recent catastrophe occurred in 1926, when a fire destroyed the main mission building. Once again the mission was reconstructed, and within three years a striking new structure rose on the site. This imposing building was modeled after an earlier Santa Clara chapel that—100 years before—was considered the "most beautiful and elaborate" church in California.

Appropriately, several objects that had been rescued from the fire were incorporated into the new structure. In fact, according to one source, more than 10,000 tiles used on the new roof had been made by Indians during the Mission Period!

Today it is that rebuilt church which greets visitors as they drive through the main gate of Santa Clara University. The history of this university goes all the way back to the 1850s, when the Franciscans turned their mission over to another order of priests, the Jesuits, for use as a college. As a result of this event, Santa Clara University enjoys the distinction of having a mission right on campus.

In addition to its location on a college campus, other features and events contribute to the uniqueness of Mission Santa Clara. Among its claims to fame is that it once had one of the largest Indian populations of the coastal chain—more than 2,200 individuals. Its inner "quad" (for "quadrangle," or court) boasts more original mission planting than any other church. Included in its gardens are perhaps the oldest and largest Banksia Rose and giant wisteria in California (and possibly the world!). Some of the olive and palm trees in the quad were planted in the 1820s—making these aged trees more than a century and a half old.

One of the most amazing events that has taken place near the mission is commemorated by a handsome marble marker in the university's gardens. It was from this spot that a giant balloon lifted off in 1905, hauling a manned glider into the air. Aboard the glider was pilot Daniel Maloney, and he was about to make aviation history.

After being lofted to the dizzying height of 4,000 feet, Maloney cut the tow rope connecting the glider to the balloon and began his daredevil ride back to earth. Along the way he wowed a crowd of spectators by executing intricate maneuvers high above the church. This historic happening has been described as "the first *controlled* flight in the United States."

As Dan Maloney sailed over the Santa Clara campus, he could look down on a tree-lined avenue known as the Alameda. Considerably older than the school, the Alameda got its start in the late 1790s. It was then that Padre Magin Catala, with the help of approximately 200 Indians, began lining the road that led to the church with trees, most of which were transplanted from the banks of a nearby river. Eventually the trees extended to the nearby pueblo, or town, of San Jose.

Founded in the same year as the mission, San Jose was the first civil settlement in California. By lining the mission road with trees, Father Catala hoped to create a pleasantly shaded avenue that would encourage people from the community to make the three- or four-mile journey to the church for Sunday mass. As the trees grew, the avenue became popular among early settlers, and not just as a way to get to church. Long-ago writers have left delightful descriptions telling about the colorfully clad people who paraded up and down the tree-lined lane.

According to some stories, Padre Catala, "the father of the Alameda," was also something of a prophet. He is said to have foretold Spain's loss of California, the influx of Americans, the discovery of gold, and even the earthquake and fire that devastated San Francisco in 1906!

Another local padre who is well remembered is Father Jose Viader. Along with Father Catala, this dedicated padre oversaw the mission for more than 30 years. Many stories are told of their long and successful reign.

One such tale about Padre Viader tells of a rough-and-tumble encounter he had with three Indians who made the mistake of attacking him. Viader's priestly robe concealed a powerful body, and he soundly thrashed his attackers. Not content to simply win the fight, Viader proceeded to lecture the threesome about their conduct. Then he promptly forgave them.

The padre's behavior so impressed one of the Indians that he became one of the mission's most dedicated supporters. Standing more than six feet in height and weighing more than 200 pounds, this formidable man dwarfed most of the other Santa Clara Valley Indians. Known to history as Marcelo, he worked long and hard for the mission, and lived to a ripe old age.

Another fight with a happy ending took place near the mission in late 1846 or early 1847, at a time when the United States and Mexico were at war. Instead of Indians and a padre, this battle pit a number of Americans against an aroused band of Mexican and Spanish Californians. The encounter was short-lived and didn't amount to much in the overall scheme of things, but it does add a splash of color to local lore.

Best known as "The Battle of Santa Clara," the spirited skirmish was also called "The Battle of the Mustard Stalks." This rather odd name fits nicely into the tale, as much of the fighting took place in an area that was covered with a head-high stand of wild mustard. Like a curtain hung behind a stage, the mustard plants created a dramatic yellow backdrop for those who watched the action from the roofs of the mission buildings. When the fighting came to an end, the rooftop spectators greeted the victorious Americans with a huge picnic dinner at the church. A few weeks later, the matter was mostly forgotten, and the warring parties were pals again.

As colorful as the Battle of the Mustard Stalks was, it had little effect on the future of the Santa Clara Valley. Far more important in the long run was a much quieter episode that had taken place at the mission about a year earlier, in 1845. There was no rooftop gallery to cheer this event, but in time it led to one of the Santa Clara area's principal claims to fame.

The story begins with a "hill of red earth" that had been known to local Indians for hundreds of years. The colored earth yielded a pigment the native Californians used as paint. So highly prized was the source of the pigment that wars are said to have been fought over it!

Some accounts indicate that the Indians used the coloring to decorate their bodies, but other sources disagree. What we do know is that they used the paint for decoration. (Among the decorated items were the walls of the original Santa Clara church.) In fact, the decorative paint was so popular that Indians from as far away as Oregon are said to have come to the area to obtain it.

For many years only the Indians seemed interested in the unusual red earth that supplied the pigment. But the story began to take a different turn in 1824, when two Spanish gentlemen built a mill on a nearby stream. These men created some excitement when they said they thought they could get silver from the red earth.

In the end the Spaniards' dreams of a silver strike proved empty. What they had actually detected—but failed identify—was quicksilver, or mercury. Nevertheless, word of their activities spread, and the name La Mina Santa Clara (The Mine of Santa Clara) became attached to the site.

The real secret of the red earth apparently remained hidden for about another 20 years. Then, in 1845, Andres Castillero, a visitor to the church, was shown a sample of the red ore. Castillero worked for the Mexican government. Among other things, he was a captain in the cavalry and an engineer. After visiting the ore site and making a few tests, he told a small group of people that he thought the deposit was quicksilver. Although not a precious metal, this silvery-white substance is valuable in its own right, and soon serious mining was begun.

As news of the discovery spread, questions began to arise concerning who had the rights to the site. A potential fortune was at stake, especially after gold was discovered in the Sierra Nevada in 1848. Because mercury is used in the reduction of gold ore, there was suddenly a huge demand for the substance. The value of the mine skyrocketed, leading to new battles—this time in the courts—over the hill of red earth that had once been the cause of Indian wars.

Together with its new fame, the old "Mine of Santa Clara" acquired a different—and appropriate—name. Perhaps the largest mercury mine in the world, an ancient site located in Spain, was called Almaden. Before long the Santa Clara find became known far and wide as New Almaden.

How rich was the mine? Certainly New Almaden became one of the world's great producers of quicksilver. By some estimates it yielded about $1 million in mercury every year. In looking over documents concerning New Almaden, it came as a surprise to me that some people considered the Indians' "hill of red earth" to be California's richest mine!

As you might have noticed in reading this book, one thing you can "bank" on is that any event involving riches will inspire a treasure trove of colorful tales. With New Almaden proving itself to be a source of vast wealth, it's not surprising that its "unofficial" history includes many stories that have become a part of local lore.

With this in mind, I'd like to share a different story about how New Almaden was discovered. This account was related to me by a man, then in his eighties, who was quite knowledgeable about the area. Appropriately enough, the tale even involves a lost treasure.

In the early 1800s, the story goes, a rich and well-known resident of San Jose was in the habit of burying his gold for safekeeping. Unfortunately, this respected citizen died without revealing the whereabouts of his vast fortune. Because it was common knowledge that he had buried his wealth, many Santa Clara Valley residents spent considerable time hunting for the treasure, without success.

As the years rolled on, hopeful treasure seekers continued to comb both likely and unlikely locations, but the site of the gold remained a mystery. According to the old man who told me this tale, it was just such a person who accidentally discovered the hill of red earth.

The discovery occurred as a vaquero, or cowboy, was exploring an area near a small, swiftly flowing stream known as Arroyo de los Alamitos (the Little River of the Poplar Trees). Keeping a sharp eye out for any sign of treasure, the rider steered his mount away from the river and toward some overhanging rocks. As he approached the rocks, intent on the ground below him, he was jumped by a large mountain lion. Falling from his rearing horse, the cowboy managed to grab his rifle, although its stock was broken in the fall. With the help of his gun and his hunting knife, he desperately fought off the snarling lion.

Badly wounded and weak from the fight, the big cat gave up its attack and tried to crawl to the nearby rocks for protection. Sadly, it could only claw at the ground feebly before it collapsed and died.

Trembling with relief at his narrow escape, the vaquero patched up his own wounds and rested a while to regain his strength. As he looked about him, he noticed that in its effort to reach the rocks the lion had exposed a portion of reddish dirt. It so happened that the vaquero had worked in his youth at the famed Almaden mine in Spain. Examining the soil uncovered by the dying lion, he was surprised to see how closely it resembled the quicksilver-rich earth he remembered from his days at Almaden.

Filling his pockets with the red dirt, the cowboy wearily began the short trip back to San Jose. After visiting a doctor, he had the soil tested—with the results known to mining buffs in most every land. As for the buried treasure the vaquero was seeking, it has never been found. Perhaps it still awaits some lucky finder in the hills near New Almaden.

Before I move on to one more treasure tale, another incident connected with New Almaden may be of interest—especially since it involves our bandit friend Tiburcio Vasquez. (Accounts of Vasquez also appear in the chapters on Missions San Gabriel, San Antonio, and Carmel.)

As with many of the gold camps that later dotted the western slope of the Sierras, the miners who arrived in the New Almaden area were soon followed by freeloaders, gamblers, troublemakers, and hangers-on. In the mid-1860s Tiburcio joined the throng and tried his hand at professional gambling. All went well until one morning when a butcher was found murdered in the nearby mining village of Enriqueta. The unfortunate butcher had been stabbed with a knife and shot in the head.

An inquest was held into the grisly crime, and because Vasquez was the only Californian in the vicinity who could speak both Spanish and English, he was sworn in as the interpreter. As it turned out, later evidence pointed to Tiburcio, and a sidekick by the name of Faustino Lorenzo, as the ones who committed the crime. But in his role as interpreter, Vasquez had little trouble "interpreting" the testimony in his own favor. As a result, the butcher was declared to have been murdered "by persons unknown." Needless to say, Tiburcio and his partner soon left the area.

Perhaps a final note concerning the life of this notorious outlaw should be included here, as it brings us back to Mission Santa Clara. As I mentioned in the chapter on Mission San Gabriel, the bandit chief was caught—for the last time—within riding distance of the San Gabriel church. Wounded in his attempt to elude capture, Vasquez spent some time in the Los Angeles jail recuperating before being transferred to the jail in San Jose. In January, 1875, he stood trial for the killing of a man during an 1873 holdup. The jury found him guilty of murder.

On March 19, 1875, Vasquez was escorted to the courtyard of the San Jose jail to face the gallows. Holding a crucifix in one hand, he calmly removed his coat, collar, and tie. A hush fell over the assembled crowd as a priest administered last rites.

At 1:35 p.m. the noose was adjusted around the convicted man's neck and a black cap placed over his head and eyes. With his last word of "Pronto!" ("Quickly!") the trap was sprung. So ended the life of one of California's most hunted badmen.

Following his execution, Vasquez was buried at the Santa Clara Mission Cemetery, a short walk from the present-day church. If you visit the Vasquez grave, you will see that the headstone is placed at an angle. According to legend, this was done to remind passers-by that the bandit had died in disrepute. However, in all probability the headstone was positioned this way because he was buried near a bend in the road.

As promised, another treasure tale is still to come. Interestingly, old-timers hint that the bonanza in question is not far from the spot where the mountain lion attacked the vaquero who was looking for a different treasure. So, when and if you feel lucky, you might want to grab your rabbit's foot (or, better yet, your metal detector) and set your sights on two stashes of hidden wealth rather than one.

The second cache is often referred to as "The Old Saddle Maker's Treasure." The saddle maker was a Frenchman named Changara. He lived on Rancho Santa Teresa (also known as the Bernal Ranch), just south of San Jose. In the early days a portion of El Camino Real passed through the ranch, and the homestead was a popular gathering place for people from miles around. Among its attractions were its bull and bear fights, its festive celebrations, and its "never failing" fresh water spring.

Changara lived in a small adobe near the Santa Teresa Spring. Also in the vicinity was a vat where he tanned hides for the saddles. (Reports indicate that part of the vat's stonework is still visible.) The Frenchman's saddles were in great demand among horsemen throughout the territory. When Changara caught up on the orders for people in and around the Santa Clara Valley, he traveled to other parts of the state to sell his handiwork. Upon returning to the ranch, the aged saddle maker supposedly buried the money he brought with him.

On one saddle-selling expedition, Changara was murdered. This cruel crime upset a great many people—and started stories about his hidden wealth.

To this day the saddle maker's treasure is still talked about by people who collect such tales. Fortune hunters from far away have tried their luck at finding the Frenchman's cache, but so far no one has reported "striking it rich" on the original Santa Teresa Ranch holdings. With much of the property now covered with buildings, I can't help but wonder whether the old saddle maker's treasure will remain lost for a long time to come.

Mission San Francisco

(Mission Dolores)

Mission San Francisco de Asis was the sixth mission to be established. It was founded in 1776 by Padre Francisco Palou (under the guidance of Padre Junipero Serra).

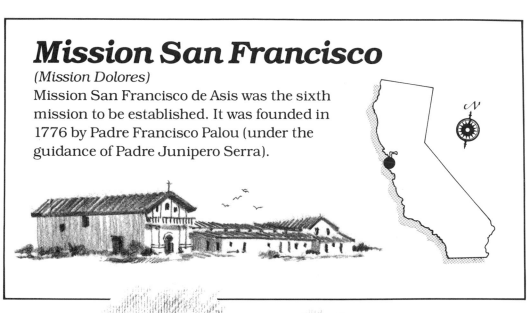

Mission San Francisco (Mission Dolores)

When Padre Francisco Palou founded Mission San Francisco de Asis, little did he know that he was planting the seed of one of the world's most charming and beautiful cities. Most historians place this historic event in late June, 1776—just a few days before the July 4 adoption of the Declaration of Independence in far-off Philadelphia marked the birth of the United States.

Some San Franciscans like to trace the history of their city back even further—all the way to 1595. It was in that year, almost two centuries before the mission was established, that the name San Francisco was first connected with the area around the Golden Gate.

Fittingly for a region that is rich in shipwreck lore, the story involves the wreck of a Spanish galleon. The ill-fated vessel was commanded by a valiant Portuguese sailor named Sebastian Rodriguez Cermenho.

Cermenho had probably earned his command during an earlier adventure on the high seas. Before his voyage to northern California, he had been the pilot of another Spanish ship that fought—and lost—a deadly Pacific duel with a craft sailing under the English flag. After relieving the badly burned galleon of its rich cargo, the victorious English put the crew ashore on a remote section of the Baja California coast and sailed away.

Despite being stranded, the Spanish were not about to give up. With the help of their pilot, Cermenho, they succeeded in sailing their crippled craft to Acapulco. Perhaps as a reward for his part in bringing the damaged vessel home, the Portuguese seafarer was made captain of his own galleon, the *San Agustin*. Unfortunately for Cermenho—not to mention his crew and the backers of his voyage—it was this ship that would meet a tragic end off a northern California shore.

Most sources agree that the mishap occurred in an inlet known today as Drake's Bay. Located approximately 30 miles north of the Golden Gate, the bay is named after Francis Drake, a daring English sea captain famous for attacking and robbing Spanish ships and settlements. Although some disagree, many people believe that Drake stopped at the bay in 1579 to recondition his ship during his famous round-the-world voyage of 1577–1580.

Sixteen years after Drake's visit is supposed to have taken place, Cermenho and the crew of the *San Agustin* were exploring the area and mapping the coastline when disaster struck. A fierce Pacific storm blew in and dashed the galleon against the rocks. The vessel—together with the load of treasure it had carried all the way from Manila in the Far East—was soon lost.

Fortunately, most of the crew were ashore when the storm hit, and they had nearly finished building a small sailing craft to use in exploring the coastal inlets. This second vessel (described by some as a launch) was not designed for ocean travel. However, with his galleon wrecked, Cermenho had no choice but to complete the smaller boat in the hope that it could carry him and his men back to Mexico.

Leaving their Oriental treasures scattered along the beach and in the depths of the bay, Cermenho and his crew crowded into the boat and resumed their voyage down the California coast. Packed in tight quarters and lashed by wind and waves, the survivors had a miserable time of it. According to one source, the lack of food only made things worse—until they came across a "big fish" that had become stranded on the rocks. Whatever this catch was, it must have been a *mighty* big fish, because the entire 70-man crew was able to live on it for a week!

Despite the hardships, Cermenho continued his original task of mapping the rugged shore, charting sections of the coast more accurately than anyone had before. Most important, he also succeeded in bringing the men to Mexico safely. Sadly, his achievements won him little praise. Instead, he was blamed for losing the galleon and its valuable cargo.

What makes this episode significant for the story of San Francisco is that the unlucky captain apparently left something besides abandoned treasure at the site of the shipwreck. Before departing for Mexico, he bestowed on the inlet the name of the Bay (or Port) of San Francisco—thus establishing the name that the region bears today.

In the decades following Cermenho's voyage, a number of vessels made their way along the northern California coast. Looking back, history buffs are amazed that for nearly 175 years after Cermenho took his leave, the beautiful harbor we know as San Francisco Bay remained undetected. Although the bay's entrance (known today as the Golden Gate) is narrow, you would think that some sharp-eyed seafarer would have spotted it eventually. But the bay remained a secret known only to the local Indians until it was discovered by the Spanish in 1769—by land!

The discovery was made by members of the Portola expedition while they were seeking the elusive bay of Monterey (as related in the Carmel Mission chapter). Usually the honor for this momentous find is given to Sargent Jose Francisco de Ortega. It was this unexpected happening that eventually led to the founding of Mission San Francisco de Asis.

Incidentally, there is an interesting anecdote about how San Francisco's first church got its name. According to the story, when Padre Serra learned that the trio of missions that were to begin the Alta California chain did not include one named in honor of St. Francis (the founder of his order), he questioned the Visitador-General, Don Jose de Galvez, about the matter. Supposedly, Galvez answered in jest, "If St. Francis desires a mission, let him cause his port to be discovered." While this tale may be more fiction than fact, I must admit that if St. Francis did have anything to do with the founding of the mission, he certainly chose a beautiful area to lend his name to.

While we are on the subject of names, I should mention that Mission San Francisco de Asis is popularly known as Mission Dolores. Apparently, the site chosen for the mission was near a small stream the Spanish called Arroyo de los Dolores (Sorrows Creek, named after Our Lady of the Sorrows). Soon a nearby lake or lagoon was also being called Dolores (Laguna de los Dolores), and in time the name was extended to the church as well. Even though the lake and the stream were filled in long ago, the name Mission Dolores persists to this day.

Another place name always comes to mind when the subject of San Francisco comes up. It is, of course, the

Golden Gate. When you hear this name, you probably think of the spectacular bridge that links the San Francisco peninsula with northern California. However, history buffs are quick to point out that the American explorer John Charles Fremont claimed to have named the entrance to San Francisco Bay in 1846—more than 90 years before the world-renowned Golden Gate Bridge was completed. The name soon took on added meaning as tens of thousands of fortune hunters passed through "the gate" on their way to the Sierra Nevada during the California Gold Rush.

When the cry of "Gold!" echoed around the world, the village that had grown up near Mission San Francisco was changed forever. Just prior to the Gold Rush, the entire population of the town (approximately 820 residents) would have fit comfortably in a modern-day school gym. The settlement boasted a pair of hotels, a couple of wharves, a newspaper, and about 200 houses. When news of "Gold for the taking!" reached the bayside village, for a time it resembled a ghost town as the locals joined the mad rush to the gold fields.

It didn't stay that way for long, though. By 1849 tens of thousands of rowdy gold seekers were finding their way to northern California. As both a Pacific gateway and a supply point, San Francisco ballooned from a small seaside settlement to an "instant city" of tents, shacks, and ramshackle buildings. By the end of 1849, its population swelled to an estimated 20,000 people. Within a dozen years, the gateway to the gold fields claimed to be the twelfth largest city in the land!

The wild and woolly days of the Gold Rush were not kind to Mission Dolores. Despite being some distance from the center of town, the aging church was not safe from the activities taking place there. Before long the neighborhood around the padres' house of prayer became noted for gambling, horse racing, saloon life, and other "unchurchlike" goings-on.

The constant stream of fortune hunters pouring into San Francisco guaranteed that the rough and ready times would continue for quite a while before things settled down. The town's port became the destination of ships from many lands. Often a cheer would rise from the decks of an incoming vessel as it cleared the Golden Gate after a long voyage. The name alone was considered good luck, and to navigate the channel safely was even better!

Gold fever seized sailors as much as everyone else, and many a multi-masted ship was abandoned by her crew after dropping anchor in San Francisco Bay. Often the ships' cargos rotted in their holds because no one could be found to unload the freight. With the dazzling vision of riches dancing in their eyes, able-bodied men had little thought for any task but digging and panning for gold in the Sierra Nevada.

So ready were the crews to leave their ships behind that at one time some 500 vessels were stranded in the bay! Instead of putting out to sea, many of these abandoned craft became part of the booming town. They were used as warehouses, hotels, lodging houses, restaurants, saloons, a jail, and—according to one source—even an insane asylum!

Some of these Gold Rush vessels are still very much a part of San Francisco—though an invisible one. They were absorbed into the landfill on which new buildings were constructed as the town expanded. Today the "bones" of these ships lie beneath the streets and skyscrapers of the city's downtown financial district!

The subject of ships' bones brings to mind the many stories of mishaps at sea that are associated with the area around Mission San Francisco. One account of a vessel that was lost near the entrance of San Francisco Bay lends even more meaning to the name "Golden" Gate.

The ship in question is known to treasure buffs as the *City of Chester*. The *Chester* burned and sank in 1888, following a collision with the steamship *Oceanic* in Pacific waters about three miles outside the Golden Gate. As with many shipwrecks, tales of sunken treasure began to circulate after the *Chester* went down. To this day the stories refuse to die—perhaps because of several accounts indicating that the *Chester* took $30 million in gold with her when she plunged to the bottom of the sea!

Coincidentally, another well-known shipwreck also involved a vessel that was named after a city. Known to many as the Queen of the China Seas, the famous steamer was officially named the *City of Rio de Janeiro,* and its loss in 1901 was one of the worst maritime disasters in California history.

The accident occurred on February 22 at about 5:40 in the morning as the Pacific Mail Steamship Company vessel attempted to enter San Francisco Bay through a dense fog. With visibility reduced by the fog and the pre-dawn darkness, an error in judgment brought the sleek ship too close to the channel's south shore. Suddenly, the crew and passengers heard the sickening sound of a shuddering, grinding crash, and the tragic last minutes of the *Rio* began to unfold.

Confusion and panic set in as those aboard the *Rio* tried to scramble to safety. Sadly, less than 20 minutes after the vessel struck the submerged rocks, all activity aboard the stricken steamer came to an abrupt end, as the gallant ship slipped beneath the sea!

Most accounts agree that there were more than 200 people aboard the *Rio* when she ran afoul of the rocks—but that fewer than 100 of them lived to talk about it. And talk they did! In fact, for many years afterward the survivors met on the anniversary of the tragedy to share their memories—and count their blessings.

In all, between 120 and 130 people perished when the *Rio* went down. Also lost, of course, was the steamer's rich cargo. Inbound from Hong Kong at the time of the wreck, the vessel was carrying a load of goods from the Orient that included such things as silk, hemp, sugar, tea, rice, opium, and tin. In addition to these goods, rumor has it that the *Rio* boasted a bonanza in silver, gold, jewelry, and other valuables.

To this day treasure buffs and diving enthusiasts continue to discuss—and search for—the lost ship and the riches that are said to have accompanied it to the ocean bottom. And who can blame them? Accounts tell of silver bullion aboard the vessel worth anywhere from $250,000 to (an exaggerated) $6 million! The rusting hulk of the *Rio* is also said to contain $75,000 in gold bullion and jewelry worth more than $37,000. Adding to the ship's lure is the question of what was in the nearly 200 bags of mail she was transporting, not to mention the hundreds of registered packages that were stored in a locked room during the fateful voyage from Hong Kong.

Although no one knows for sure how much treasure the Queen of the China Seas was carrying, estimates of its value range from less than $500,000 all the way up to $11 million! Even if the amounts have become exaggerated over the years, it's little wonder that the wreck of the *Rio* is a favorite topic of discussion among divers and fans of sunken treasure.

Another reason for the continued interest in the lost steamer, at least among treasure buffs, is that the *Rio* is said to have sunk close to shore. Some accounts state that the site of the wreck was in the vicinity of Fort Point, at a location that today is almost directly under the Golden Gate Bridge. With this in mind, you would think the ship's remains would be relatively easy to locate. But despite a handful of reported finds, to date no one has proved a claim of finding either the *Rio* or her cargo.

When the Spanish selected a site near San Francisco
Bay for their sixth mission outpost, they guaranteed that
tales of shipwrecks—and lost treasure—would become part of
the lore of the future settlement. But not all of San Francisco's treasure tales concern the treacherous waters around
the Golden Gate. In fact, a number of other bonanzas are
said to be buried closer to the downtown area and the mission itself.

Appropriately enough, one such cache was hidden—
and lost—in the heart of the area that became the city's
financial district. This episode had its beginning when two
women arrived in San Francisco in 1850. Like many newcomers, the ladies were temporarily sheltered in a tent.
Frightened by the many unruly characters who frequented
the neighborhood, they became concerned about the safety
of their valuables. Among their belongings were Mexican
doubloons, gold nuggets, precious jewels, and deeds to large
land holdings in southern California. To keep these items
safe, they decided to bury them near their tent until they
found a more secure place to live.

After finding more permanent accommodations in
another part of the city, the two women took some time to
settle in before returning to their original quarters to retrieve
their fortune. Much to their dismay, when they did go back to
where their tent had been, they found stacks of stone piled
on the site and a lot of construction going on. Their pleas to
move the piles of rock fell on deaf ears, and before long a
large building rose on the very spot where the treasure lay
concealed. There the cache remained, buried under tons of
concrete, for 76 years.

In 1926 it was announced that the structure that had covered the women's fortune would be demolished. When the building came down, a son of one of the women was on hand to reclaim the long-lost wealth. Unfortunately, when he searched the site, he found nothing at all! Perhaps, as the son believed, he was beaten to the treasure by a steamshovel scooping up the earth beneath the building, and the valuables were dumped into a truck along with the dirt and hauled away.

As I wander the streets of San Francisco today, I can't help but wonder how many other treasures might have been built upon over the years. Most of them, of course, would have been buried by people, but it may come as a surprise that Mother Nature also had a hand in spreading the wealth.

As a matter of fact, while many early San Franciscans rushed off to the Sierra Nevada in their quest for gold, they might have had a bit of luck if they had looked for the yellow metal in their own backyards. Tales of gold being found in the city's famous hills began circulating as early as the 1850s, and at least five locations of reported gold strikes are within easy walking distance of the mission (the farthest being about three miles away). Unfortunately, it wouldn't do any good for me to tell you where these sites are, for today they are all covered by buildings, pavement, and streets.

Another treasure tale that is especially fitting for this chapter involves both a shipwreck and a church treasure associated with Mission Dolores. This story also introduces one of the picturesque islands of San Francisco Bay.

The tale begins about the time the Mexican government took control of the California missions in the 1830s. As related in an earlier chapter, during this time the padres at many of the coastal churches took precautions to keep their valuables from falling into the wrong hands. According to local legend, the fathers at Mission Dolores decided to place their church's treasures in large chests and load them aboard a ship bound for Spain.

Unfortunately, the vessel never reached its destination. In fact, it never even made it out of San Francisco Bay! Instead, as the sloop headed for the Golden Gate, a storm came up and dashed it against the north coast of Yerba Buena Island (now a midway point for the San Francisco–Oakland Bay Bridge). Luckily, the chests were recovered from the wreck. Supposedly, they were then buried on the island, where they remain to this day.

The church treasure, by the way, isn't the only hoard of valuables that is said to be stashed on Yerba Buena Island. According to another tale, some years after the mission chests were buried, an American whaling vessel made a stop at San Francisco on its way to the north Pacific. Unlike most whalers, this vessel was carrying a treasure—one it had acquired in a most unusual way.

The ship's previous port of call had been Callao, Peru. While it was anchored in the harbor, a revolution broke out. In the midst of the unrest, a small group of wealthy Peruvians approached the captain and pleaded with him to store their valuables aboard his vessel for safekeeping. Thinking the revolution would soon be over, the captain agreed.

Unfortunately for the rich Peruvians, when it came time for the ship to leave, the uprising was still in progress. Unable to wait any longer, the captain sailed out of the harbor with the wealth still on board. Different sources give different viewpoints concerning the captain's intentions. Some say he planned to return the treasure on his next trip to Peru, while others indicate he planned to keep the valuables for himself.

Whatever the captain's plans were, he was wise enough to know that whaling and treasure don't mix. So, when the ship put in at San Francisco, he decided to "bank" the wealth in a safe place before heading for the Arctic. Along with selected members of his crew, he loaded the valuables onto a small boat and rowed them to the Yerba Buena shore. From there the men took the treasure inland and buried it.

Soon afterward the whaler took leave of San Francisco. This should be the end of the story, as the vessel was never heard from again. However, even though we may be able to write "the end" to the captain and most of his crew, the treasure tale isn't quite finished yet. According to one source, a member of the crew jumped ship before it sailed out of the Golden Gate. This sailor was one of the shipmates who had helped to bury the bonanza, and it was he who later told the story of the treasure stash.

At this point you might think that we could write "the end" to the treasure too, as it would seem that the sailor would simply have uncovered the valuables and enjoyed whatever pleasures they could buy. Apparently, however, this was not the case. It seems that the men who took part in hiding the hoard were all made to swear a "terrible oath" of secrecy. Being a man of honor—not to mention afraid of what would become of him if he broke his word—the man kept the secret of the treasure's location until the day he died. So, if we can believe this account, perhaps the wealth of several Peruvian families is still hidden on Yerba Buena Island!

Incidentally, in 1939 the Golden Gate International Exposition (the second of San Francisco's world fairs) opened on a man-made island that adjoins Yerba Buena. During the construction of this island, countless tons of dirt and rock were transported to the site. With this in mind, some have speculated that perhaps the treasures that were on Yerba Buena got mixed in with this fill. If so, maybe there is more to the name of the artificial isle than most people realize—for it is called by one and all Treasure Island!

In closing this chapter on Mission Dolores, I would like to mention some treasures of another kind—ones that can be found by anyone who cares to visit the historic mission grounds. These treasures are not gold or silver or precious jewels, but common stone. To many they may seem to be worth little, but to history buffs like me they are priceless, for they help us to relive the fabulous history of the city that grew up around the Spanish mission.

The treasures I am thinking of are the grave markers that dot the mission's cemetery. To stroll through the small garden, reading the inscriptions on the markers, is to walk back in time. In the silence of the graveyard we can acquaint ourselves with some of the people who helped build one of America's favorite cities. There are names that we remember from history books (such as Don Luis Antonio Arguello, one of California's early governors), and there are names that perhaps no one remembers. There are winners and losers, young and old, rich and poor, famous and infamous. There are native Californians resting alongside those who were native to lands far across the sea.

Maybe it is this mixture of people that helps to make this final resting place so special. Like San Francisco itself, the mission graveyard is home to individuals of many kinds, colors, nationalities, and places of origin, all brought together by the tides of history to the beautiful city by the bay.

Author's Notes

Each book in the **History & Happenings of California Series** has an Author's Notes section providing background information and additional points of interest about the **people, places,** and **events** mentioned in the text. While I hope that these notes provide valuable tidbits for all readers, the facts presented here may be especially useful to students and teachers in enriching reports and classroom discussions.

In writing this book, I have not tried to duplicate the many books that detail the history of the Mission Period or explore the controversies surrounding the European settlement of California. Instead, my purpose has been to present colorful and often little-known tales that can lead young readers to various aspects of the fascinating history—and enduring legacy—of California's coastal churches. As a fourth-grade teacher for 15 years, I found that once students were hooked by a tale of banditry, shipwreck, or lost treasure, they could begin to chart their own explorations and pursue the subject in any direction that interested them.

In a book of this size, there is room to tell only a fraction of the tantalizing tales related to California's missions. To keep the book to a manageable size, I decided to select seven missions from different parts of California whose stories are representative of mission lore. Fans of the remaining 14 establishments can rest assured that each has its own tales and treasures associated with it! Perhaps in a future book (or two) I will be able to share some of them.

Included in this book's sampling of stories are some that dwell in a shadowy place somewhere between legend and established fact. One of these is the tale that opens the Introduction, telling of the **trail of mustard seeds** left by the padres along the El Camino Real. What does seem to be well-established is that some of the mustard plants so common in present-day California were indeed introduced to the area by European explorers and settlers. In particular, the padres are said to have cultivated mustard in their mission gardens. Many believe that it was from these gardens that the seed was scattered into the wild, perhaps being carried on occasion by the padres themselves as they tramped along the King's Road.

It may have been this "seed" of truth that gave rise to the legend of mustard plants blossoming each spring to mark the path between the missions with a blaze of yellow. In any case, in various versions the charming story is an old and cherished part of California lore.

Speaking of the **El Camino Real,** the path between the churches is often thought of as having stretched from California's southernmost mission, San Diego, to its northernmost counterpart in Sonoma (Mission San Francisco Solano). However, some sources suggest that the original El Camino Real was much longer, reaching from Sonoma to Mexico City— and from there all the way to Guatemala!

The modern highway known to Californians as El Camino Real closely follows the original path in some places, but in others it is a considerable distance from the padres' mission trail. To complicate matters, there may not have been a single path between certain missions. Instead, at different times, various routes may have been used by padres, Indians, and other travelers.

One must assume that there were several paths that led to and from **Mission San Diego,** the earliest of Alta California's churches and the subject of the first chapter of this book. One such route led to the Baja California mission of Santa Catalina. It was this trail that brought to San Diego the unwelcome Yankee visitors **Sylvester Pattie** and his young son, **James Ohio Pattie.** As related in the chapter, the Patties pioneered a new route to the coast before their harsh (and, for Sylvester, fatal) experience in San Diego. The trail they blazed to California is often referred to as the Gila River Route.

The book written by the younger Pattie after his return to the United States was called *Personal Narrative.* Even though parts of this work are exaggerated, most agree that it contains valuable information and is exciting to read. Incidentally, youthful readers might like to know that James Ohio Pattie was only about 15 years old when he embarked upon his great adventure.

Following the Pattie account, the San Diego chapter relates a couple of tales of **ships lost in desert sands.** Although such an event might seem improbable, there are other, similar stories told about the same general area.

As an example, one of these stories involves a boat that was built in Los Angeles in 1862. The people who backed the building of this vessel were planning to travel to La Paz, Arizona, in search of gold. Their plan was to transport the boat by wagon across the desert and use it to cross the Colorado River on their way to La Paz. Unfortunately, the expedition ended in disaster far from its destination when the team pulling the cumbersome wagon bogged down in the desert sand. The boat had to be abandoned where it lay, perhaps to be covered and uncovered over the years as the sands shifted.

The San Diego chapter also tells of ships lost in more traditional locations, such as the Spanish galleons *Trinidad* and *Santo Domingo.* Shipwreck enthusiasts may wish to note that, according to one well-researched source, more than 25 such vessels met their end in California waters.

Considerable uncertainty surrounds the fate of the *Trinidad.* Most accounts indicate that the vessel was lost around 1540, but there is less agreement on the question of where she went down. Over the years divers claim to have found evidence of the vessel in different locations. The consensus of opinion seems to be that she was lost somewhere between La Jolla (slightly north of San Diego) and Oceanside (farther up the coast).

In regard to Mission San Diego itself, among the notable features of this early church were a school, a thriving vineyard, and an irrigation system. In time its pluses also included a more elaborate church, dedicated in 1813 (and, like its predecessor, located several miles from the original mission site). This church has since been restored and may be visited today.

The mission's impressive water system included an imposing dam, completed in 1816 and described as part of California's first irrigation and engineering system. Remains of the dam are visible to this day. The site is a National Historic Landmark and can be reached by way of the Old Mission Gorge Road.

Those who have become interested in the story of Mission San Diego's "little sister," **Santa Ysabel,** may wish to know that in the 1920s a new church was built near the site of the original chapel. It is located on Highway 79, about a mile and a half north of the community of Santa Ysabel.

Our second chapter takes us northward to **Mission San Gabriel.** Fittingly enough, considering its location near the future "City of the Angels," this church was named after an archangel. In the early days, the prosperous establishment was also referred to as the Queen of the Missions, a title that today is most often applied to Mission Santa Barbara.

In thinking about early place names in this region, I'm reminded that one of my favorites is **Rio de los Temblores** (River of the Earthquakes). This title certainly proved to be prophetic, as earthquakes have continued to shake things up from time to time ever since. The quakes that seem to have done the most damage to the mission occurred between 1803 and 1812. Among other things, these temblors ruined the church roof and toppled the bell towers.

With several accounts of California badman **Tiburcio Vasquez** in this chapter, I should mention that—as with other famous personalities of the Old West—many more tales are told about this notorious outlaw (and his treasures of bandit loot) than are likely to be true. But there is no denying that Vasquez himself was very real—as was the eagerness of lawmen to catch up with him! Incidentally, there is some doubt about the exact location where the bandit was captured for the last time, with sources indicating that he was caught either in the Santa Monica foothills or closer to what is now downtown Hollywood. Either way, most would agree that the location was within a short ride of San Gabriel Mission.

With outlaws on my mind, I should add that **Joaquin Murrieta,** California's number one badman, is also said to have frequented the San Gabriel area . . . to visit his sister.

Next on our list is stately **Mission Santa Barbara,** the reigning "Queen of the Missions." You may recall that Joaquin Murrieta makes an appearance in this chapter also, in the story of the planting of the grapevine. Although the bandit's grapevine is said to have been located near the church, it is possible that it was instead planted a considerable distance away. For an interesting account of this episode, ask anyone who is familiar with the history of Grapevine Canyon (or Creek) in the San Rafael Wilderness area (north of the mission).

Of all the many stories told about this regal church, however, my favorite by far is the account of **Juana Maria,** the lonely lady of San Nicolas.

Certainly this remarkable woman was a queen in her own right. In fact, as the absolute monarch of her island home, she could have chosen any title she wished. Today visitors to the mission cemetery often stop to read the plaque on the wall that honors her memory. The remembrance was placed there by the Santa Barbara chapter of the Daughters of the American Revolution in 1928.

Interestingly, as with Old Gabriel (whose story is told in the chapter on Carmel Mission), Juana Maria's fame eventually reached all the way to the church headquarters in Rome. After her death, one of the garments she had fashioned for herself—an exquisite robe made out of cormorant feathers—was put on display in the Vatican Museum.

The tides of history often produce strange ironies, as is illustrated by the continuing story of the island on which Juana Maria spent all those lonely years, fearful of harsh treatment by otter hunters. Today the island is once again in the news—this time because a breeding colony for the once-imperiled sea otter is being established there. So, the furry little fellows that lured hunters to the island long ago are now attracting people who are trying to ensure the creatures' survival.

Continuing our northward trek, the next chapter takes up the tale of **Mission San Antonio.** Situated more than 20 miles from the nearest main highway, and located within the confines of a military post, San Antonio attracts fewer visitors than most of the other establishments in the mission chain. But its relative obscurity only adds to the air of mystery surrounding this secluded church.

Much of the early success of Mission San Antonio must be credited to a man I did not mention in the text, Padre Buenaventura Sitjar. This remarkable individual labored at the church from its founding in 1771 to his death 37 years later. Even allowing for the short break that occurred in the late 1790s, when Father Sitjar helped establish neighboring Mission San Miguel, his period of service at San Antonio was one of the longest in the history of the Mission Period.

Included in the many achievements of this dedicated and observant padre was the writing of a book that recorded the vocabulary and grammar of the Indians of the San Antonio area. Today this priceless document is preserved in the Smithsonian Institution in Washington, D.C.

Among San Antonio's distinctions, according to certain sources, is that it was the first Alta California church to use the now-familiar Spanish-style roof tiles. The fame of the mission's tiles was enhanced when some of them were displayed at the San Francisco Midwinter Fair in 1894. Sadly, instead of being returned to the mission—which was in a state of decay at the time—several hundred of the tiles reportedly ended up on the roof of the Southern Pacific Railroad station in the San Francisco suburb of Burlingame.

Moving north and west from San Antonio, we come to the second church founded by the padres in Alta California, known to most people today as **Carmel Mission.** This church was first known as Mission San Carlos Borromeo and was originally located in Monterey. However, Padre Junipero Serra soon realized that the original site left much to be desired. Not only did a number of the soldiers at the Monterey Presidio attempt to lead certain Indians astray (in Serra's eyes), but the lack of fertile land and fresh water hindered his long-range plans for the church. In 1771 the mission was moved about five miles south to its present location near the Carmel River (and the beautiful Carmel Bay and Carmel Valley).

The question of how the name Carmel came to be associated with the area has been debated by historians for many years. Several accounts suggest that the name goes back to 1602, when the Basque seafarer and explorer **Sebastian Vizcaino** planted the Spanish banner on the Monterey shore. According to these stories, Vizcaino bestowed the name Carmelo on a local mountain and its valley, either because he was reminded of the Bible's Mount Carmel or because he wanted to honor his patron saint, Our Lady of Carmel. A third story says that he permitted two Carmelite friars who made the trip with him to name the valley El Carmelo in honor of their order.

However, another traditional story claims that it was **Padre Junipero Serra** who was responsible for the Carmel name. According to this tale, it was Serra who saw a mountain to the south of the Monterey Peninsula that reminded him of the Holy Land's Mount Carmel. When he moved his mission from its original location in Monterey, Serra picked a spot near this mountain and bestowed the name Carmelo on the area, including the mountain, the fertile valley below, and a nearby fresh-water stream.

Whichever is the true account, to this day the church is officially known as Mission San Carlos Borromeo del Rio Carmelo (the Mission of Saint Charles Borromeo of the Carmel River).

Whether or not Vizcaino had anything to do with the name Carmel, he does get credit for naming the location that would become the site of California's first capital city. The members of his expedition in 1602 were the first Europeans to set foot on the shores of **Monterey Bay.** So impressed was Vizcaino with the peaceful harbor that he named it after the man who was responsible for his voyage—the Viceroy of New Spain, the Count de Monte Rey.

Of course, the future capital city did not actually get its start until June 3, 1770, when Padre Serra and **Gaspar de Portola** met to offer their prayers of thanksgiving in the shade of a mighty oak tree on the Monterey shore. Most people are unaware that this aged tree became one of the most historic in the United States—and not only because it sheltered the spot where the presidio and mission were officially founded. It was under the branches of the very same tree that, more than a century and a half earlier, Vizcaino and his crew had gathered and unfurled the Spanish flag for the first time in this part of California. Today, visitors to Carmel Mission's excellent museum can see part of the Pacific Coast's historic Vizcaino Oak.

Those who visit the Monterey Peninsula may also notice large wooden crosses on the shores of Monterey and Carmel bays (the Carmel Bay cross is only a short distance from the mission). The two crosses commemorate those that were erected by the Portola party in 1769.

Moving on to the topic of **Joaquin Murrieta,** California's best-known badman, I should mention that there is considerable controversy concerning his death. In fact, even though the California Rangers were rewarded for killing the desperado, many of those who knew Murrieta personally only chuckled at the claim that the outlaw was dead. Interestingly, one individual who has extensively researched the bandit king's life and death suggests that the man whom the Rangers killed—and passed off as Murrieta—was actually an Indian named Chappo who was raised at Mission San Carlos!

The chapter also talks about a "bandit" of the sea, **Hippolyte de Bouchard.** Although not technically a pirate, Bouchard is often pinned with that label. In any case, his attack on Monterey made it the only community in the Golden State that has ever been sacked by a buccaneer of this type.

As a final note on this chapter, I should point out that church officials question some of the tales of lost treasure that are part of the lore of Carmel Mission. In comparing aged inventories with what the mission still has in store, they say that all items are accounted for—with many of them in use to this day.

Among the things worth remembering about our next church, **Mission Santa Clara,** is that it was one of the most prosperous missions of the coastal chain. Perhaps equally important from the padres' point of view, approximately 8,500 Indian baptisms took place there. This impressive figure was tops among Alta California's early churches.

As I noted in the text, the mission was not without its difficult times and in fact had to be rebuilt on several occasions. Incidentally, in 1781 a cornerstone was laid for what was to become Santa Clara's third church. Long forgotten, the cornerstone was accidentally dug up in 1911 by a crew laying a gas line. Other items were uncovered as well—including coins, crucifixes, and medals—and are now on display at the Santa Clara University museum.

Dan Maloney's historic flight above the college at Santa Clara is one of the highlights of the area's later history. Although Maloney piloted the frail craft, much of the credit must go to the glider's designer, John Joseph Montgomery. Considered by some to be the "father" of controlled flight, Montgomery was among the first to understand the laws of aerodynamics. By the way, he taught at Santa Clara College, the institution that was built around the mission (and that has since become known as **Santa Clara University**).

In reference to the skirmish involving the feisty **Father Viader,** one account I came across indicated that there were only two attackers, rather than the three reported in most sources. The exact number probably isn't important now, but you can bet it made a difference then!

Those who are aware that there is also a Mission San Jose may wonder about the connection between Santa Clara and the town of **San Jose.** California's first civil settlement, the pueblo of San Jose was established in the same year (1777) as the Santa Clara church. Mission San Jose came along some 20 years later and is not nearly as close to the present-day city of San Jose as is Mission Santa Clara.

South of the Santa Clara church is the site of the **New Almaden mine.** While different sources credit various individuals with the mine's discovery, there is no doubt that the find was one of the most significant in California's mining history. Incidentally, if the story of New Almaden has aroused your interest, you may want to take a trip to the site, as there is still much to see. Most maps of Santa Clara County will show you the route. Remember, though, that permission must be obtained before certain areas are explored.

Our final chapter samples the rich history of the area surrounding **Mission San Francisco de Asis.** The location of this church near San Francisco Bay ensured that a colorful history would follow, for the entrance to the wind-swept bay was bound to become a primary gateway for newcomers to the Golden State.

There is some question concerning who deserves the honor of being the first European to spot the bay. Although the credit usually goes to the men of the Portola expedition in 1769, it is possible that the discovery was made almost two centuries earlier by the English adventurer **Francis Drake** and his crew. As indicated in the chapter, Drake stopped along the northern California coast to recondition his ship in 1579. Some argue that the landing took place somewhere other than Drake's Bay. Among other possible landing sites is an inlet near Point San Quentin, within the confines of San Francisco Bay. If this was, in fact, where Drake made landfall, then it is the English sea captain and his men who should be known as the non-Indian "discoverers" of this beautiful harbor.

Incidentally, in light of the uncertainty concerning the exact location of Drake's landing, perhaps "his" bay should be renamed Cermenho's Bay. Most historians do agree that this location was where the Portuguese captain lost his ship and its Oriental treasures in 1595.

While we're on the subject of names, I should note that not everyone agrees with **John Charles Fremont's** claim to having named the **Golden Gate.** Some sources suggest that Francis Drake may have christened the entranceway to San Francisco Bay with the very same name more than 260 years before Fremont arrived on the scene!

Whether it was Drake or Fremont who first referred to the bay's entrance as the Golden Gate, I'm sure neither of them could have foreseen what that name would mean to the tens of thousands of gold seekers who passed through the channel on their way to the Sierra Nevada. For these eager argonauts, the Gate indeed was "golden"—at least in their dreams!

Another name that has long been connected with San Francisco is Yerba Buena (good herb). In fact, the village that was located where a portion of downtown San Francisco now stands went by that name until 1847. In case you're wondering, the "good herb" for which the town was originally named is described as a white-flowered wild mint that grew in the region.

Among the many shipwreck stories connected with the San Francisco area, the tale of the ***City of Rio de Janeiro*** is one of the most dramatic—and one of the most puzzling, since the ship seems to have disappeared without a trace. One avid history buff and retired sea captain has proposed a novel theory to explain what became of the wreck. The captain suggests that the *Rio*'s 334-foot bulk might have been swept into an underwater cavern near Fort Point—and then covered up in the settling of the earth following the famous 1906 San Francisco earthquake (which took place about five years after the loss of the *Rio*). If the captain's explanation is right, the treasure-laden ship may be resting in her own private chamber beneath Fort Point, sealed off forever by the mighty quake of '06.

In this connection, I must note that when it comes to the lives and treasure lost in shipwrecks, one often finds very different numbers in various sources. In fact, I happened to talk to a California shipwreck diver while I was preparing these notes, and he indicated that he thinks portions of the *Rio* have been found—and that the value of her treasure has been greatly exaggerated over the years.

Those who are curious about **Fort Point** may be interested to know that a military outpost was first built on the San Francisco peninsula's north shore in the late 1700s. This Spanish establishment was eventually taken over by Mexico, and then by the United States. The fort we see today was built by the United States in the mid-1800s. Although dwarfed by the Golden Gate Bridge, it is still an impressive structure and a fascinating place to visit. Fort Point is open to the public as part of the Golden Gate National Recreation Area.

I hope those who have become interested in the history—and legacy—of California's missions will make it a point to visit these aged relics of the state's colorful past, as well as the many historic sites like Fort Point that came to be built near them. In closing, however, I would like to mention that there is much more to our state's history than is preserved in buildings and other structures. In particular, let me end with a tip of the hat to the region's original inhabitants, the **California Indians** who saw their land become a magnet for wave after wave of people from all points of the globe. It was their ancestors who were the true discoverers of the territory that would become the Golden State. Since these first immigrants came to California, our rich and varied land has been "discovered" again and again by people seeking a better life—and no doubt it will continue to be rediscovered for ages to come.

About the Author

Randall A. Reinstedt was born and raised on California's beautiful and historic Monterey Peninsula. After traveling widely throughout the world, he spent fifteen years teaching elementary school students, with special emphasis on California and local history. Today he continues to share his love of California's beauty and lore with young and old alike through his immensely popular publications. Among his many books is **More Than Memories: History & Happenings of the Monterey Peninsula**, an acclaimed history text for fourth-graders that is used in schools throughout the Monterey area.

Randy lives with his wife, Debbie, in a house overlooking the Pacific Ocean. In addition to his writing projects, he is in great demand as a lecturer on regional history to school and adult groups, and he frequently gives workshops for teachers on making history come alive in the classroom.

About the Illustrator

A native Californian, Ed Greco has spent most of his professional career as a graphic designer and illustrator. Born and raised in the Santa Clara Valley, Ed grew up studying and illustrating northern California, its environment, and its history.

Randall A. Reinstedt's
History & Happenings of California Series

Through colorful tales drawn from the rich store of California lore, this series introduces young readers to the historical heritage of California and the West. "Author's Notes" at the end of each volume provide information about the people, places, and events encountered in the text. Whether read for enjoyment or for learning, the books in this series bring the drama and adventure of yesterday to the young people of today.

Currently available in both hardcover and softcover:

Lean John, California's Horseback Hero

One-Eyed Charley, the California Whip

Otters, Octopuses, and Odd Creatures of the Deep

Stagecoach Santa

The Strange Case of the Ghosts of the Robert Louis Stevenson House

Tales and Treasures of California's Missions

Tales and Treasures of the California Gold Rush

Hands-On History teacher resource books are available to accompany titles in the **History & Happenings of California Series.** Packed with projects and activities integrating skills across the curriculum, these imaginative resource books help bring California history to life in the classroom.

For information about the **History & Happenings of California Series,** *as well as other titles by Randy Reinstedt for both children and adults, please write:*

GHOST TOWN PUBLICATIONS
P. O. Drawer 5998
Carmel, CA 93921